CREATIVE SOFT TOY MAKING

by Pamela Peake

Thanks and appreciation are extended to all my
friends who have helped in so many ways to give
me the freedom to design and make toys. I am
also indebted to the many individuals who have
encouraged me, particularly the ladies of the
Women's Institute. I hope they like the results.
While to my family there is a very special thank-
you for their indulgence and understanding.

to Susan and Katherine

CREATIVE SOFT TOY MAKING

by Pamela Peake

Bobbs-Merrill

Indianapolis / New York

Contents

Colour Illustrations

Preface

Soft toys occupy a rather unique place amongst all the toys that a child will play with. They are companions, comforters, and confidants, ultimately becoming nostalgic reminders of childhood, if indeed they survive the process of playing.

In the past, inspiration for designing soft toys frequently came from a limited number of animals in the immediate environment of the child. Today, however, there are no such boundaries; even time is no barrier, for prehistoric animals make very popular toys. To answer a child's or an adult's request for a special character, or produce a happy surprise, is indeed an achievement.

All the basic information needed for soft toy making is given in the first few chapters, for an understanding of what you are trying to do will undoubtedly help you to make successful toys. The instructions and patterns are arranged in groups that reflect either style or subject. With careful working, you should be able to start wherever you wish, although it would be wise to proceed cautiously if you are a newcomer to this ancient craft.

Notes

If at any time you have difficulty in obtaining items for toys, such as eyes or musical units, you can order them by mail from the following companies:

In Britain:

The Needlewoman,
146–8 Regent Street,
London W1R 6BA

Fred Aldous Ltd.,
P.O. Box 135,
37 Lever Street,
Manchester M60 1UX

Both of these companies supply a catalogue for a small fee.

In the United States:

Dollspart Supply Company, Inc., 5–06 51st Avenue, Long Island City, N.Y. 11101

glass eyes; music boxes, Mama voices; regular and spray-on paint; stuffing tools, glues.

Standard Doll Company, 23–83 31st Street, Long Island City, N.Y. 11105

glass eyes, paste-on and sew-on wiggle eyes; music boxes, Mama and crying voices, squeakers; Dacron Polyester stuffing material, foam-plastic cones and other shapes; fabrics, felt, lace and embroidery edgings, braid; glues.

Lee Wards, 1200 St. Charles Street, Elgin, Illinois 60120

paste-on and sew-on movable, rolling, and blinking eyes; Dacron Polyester stuffing material, styrofoam cones and other shapes; acrylic paints, ballpoint 'embroidery' paint; fabrics, felt, lace edgings, braid; glues.

fur and fur fabrics: either fur or a fur fabric, according to your own preference, can be used to make any of the furry toys in this book.

metric measurements: metric equivalents are given to the nearest half centimetre. Yardages are given to the nearest centimetre.

eg.   3″ = 7·5cm
6″ = 15cm
1 yd = 91cm

I Materials and Methods

Fabrics, patterns, and sound workmanship are the necessary ingredients for successful toy-making. To help you achieve this, the opening chapters provide all the information and instructions needed for making the toys in this book, as well as the basis for developing your toymaking further.

Fabrics

Fabrics are characterized by a number of different properties, the most obvious being colour, texture, and design. These features, either separately or combined, provoke different responses in the eye of the beholder, and obviously the most successful is the combination that has the strongest appeal.

Certain toys, like the soft cuddly toys for very young children, demand a particular type of fabric. These are more successful if made in furry fabrics, whose characteristics are their very soft texture, pastel colours, and suitability for washing. In contrast, pandas, tigers, and zebras can only be recognized by colour and colour patterns and these must be incorporated into the making of the toy. Colour can also enhance character, for white and pastel shades are frequently used to denote softness and youthfulness, while reds, emeralds, and other bold colours may suggest aggressiveness. The aniline dyes used in modern fabrics produce many abrasive colours that again influence the appeal of a toy.

The universal appeal of teddy bears can be attributed to the attractive colours and texture of fabric used, plus an appealing shape. The texture has always been soft and cuddly, although recently this has been further enhanced by the use of very long pile fur fabrics to produce a 'super bear' texture. Colours have been varied but the majority have always been the warm hues of honey, gold, rust, and cinnamon. For the babies there have been whites and pastel colours. The use of dark colours and even blacks has been restricted to the more sophisticated bears for older children. Colours for toys tend to follow fashionable trends and no longer is realism the most important criterion. Experiments in colour and pattern are constantly being produced in modern fabrics and these should provide a unique challenge to the ingenuity of the toy-maker.

For toys that are recognized by shape only, the choice of fabrics is much greater. They should provide additional interest and help to ensure a favourable response to the character. Nevertheless, the wrong choice or combination of fabrics can equally well detract from the toy. When choosing fabric, one must also consider its strength and therefore suitability for hard wear and tear. Lightweight dressmaking cottons are best reserved for dolls' clothes, while heavier weight woollens and other firm woven dress fabrics can be used for making the toy skins. I prefer to use furnishing weight cottons and upholstery fabrics as they are manufactured with such gay colours and patterns as well as interesting textures. Fabrics which fray easily, have a shiny surface, bold patterns of stripes, checks and spots, or are constructed to allow stretch, are all difficult to use and are best avoided until you have gained considerable experience.

The following chart provides a guide to the more commonly used materials.

Fabrics and Fibres	Fabric Characteristics
Cotton fabrics	All made with natural fibre from the cotton plant seed pod. Includes the lightweight lawns, ginghams, Madras, muslin, poplin, and Oxford cloths. Heavier qualities are canvas, calico, ticking, denim, corduroy, and velveteen.
Plissé and Seersucker	Textured cottons with a crinkled surface.
Denim	Fabric with coloured threads running in lengthwise direction (warp) and white threads running in the crosswise direction (weft). Treat this fabric as napped.
Corduroy	A cotton fabric with pile arranged in prominent ribs. Modern corduroy is ribless, sculptured, printed, and even quilted. It is still a napped fabric and is best cut with nap running down the fabric.
Terry towelling	Cotton fabric with loops on one or both sides. Treat as a napped fabric.
Velveteen	Cotton fabric made to look like velvet. Treat as a napped fabric.
Acrilan, Courtelle, Orlon, and Dralon	These synthetic fabrics are made from acrylic fibres. They compete with wool for softness and warmth. Not attacked by moth grubs or beetles; non-felting, quick-drying, easy-care fabrics. Used for making knitted fabrics, washable tweeds, and imitation furs.
Bouclé	Term used to describe fabric made from bouclé yarn. This yarn has loops and knots in it so that it provides a rough surface texture. Usually made from a woollen fibre.
Tweed	Fabric with a rough, unfinished appearance. Traditionally made with wool fibres, but modern tweeds have acrylic fibres. Tweeds can be patterned, some very distinctively, like Houndstooth and Herringbone.
Angora	Fabric made from hair of Angora rabbit. It is warm, soft, and very fluffy.
Mohair	Long pile fabric made from hair of the Angora goat. Fabric may be coloured, patterned, and woven in several ways.
Velvet	A plain or patterned fabric with a thick cut pile providing a smooth texture. Originally made from silk but now made with rayon, acetate, nylon, and cotton fibres. It is a napped fabric with the nap running upwards for the richest and darkest colour.

Furs	These may be either natural or artificial. Natural furs have no grain. Artificial furs have a deep pile, less dense than the pile of velvet. The fabrics may be either woven or knitted and the fibres most commonly used are the acrylics and modacrylics. Remember that knitted fur has a tendency to stretch. Treat artificial furs as napped fabrics.
Teklan	This fabric is made from modacrylic fibres. It is strong, hard wearing, and more important, is flame proof. Used in imitation furs.
Felt	Felt is a non-woven, non-knitted fabric. It is made by matting fibres together. It therefore has no grain, can be cut in any direction, and does not fray. There are over 150 plain colours to choose from.

Equipment

All the sewing aids that are used for dressmaking could be needed at some time for your toymaking. These include scissors, pinking shears, needles, pins, cottons, tailor's chalk, tape measure, and sewing machine. Apart from these you will also need the following items, but remember there are frequently satisfactory alternatives. For example, instead of using a pair of compasses, draw around a cup or plate.

General

Linen button thread for closing openings
Powder or silicone spray for sewing through foam
Latex glue for fabric
Glue for card and paper
Brushes and vacuum cleaner for final grooming

For pattern making

Squared (graph) paper or large sheets of plain paper
Tracing or detail paper
Pencils and ruler
Set square with right angle
Pair of compasses
Thin card
Paper scissors

For stuffing

Toothpicks, wooden meat skewers, and dowelling rods as stuffing sticks
Forceps

For embroidery

Assorted needles
Assorted embroidery threads
Sequins and beads

For jointing

Thin, round-nosed pliers
Steel knitting needle

For inserting wired eyes and noses

Wire cutters
Thin, round-nosed pliers
Steel knitting needle
Long darning needle or upholsterer's 8″ needle

For inserting safety lock in eyes and noses

The special fixing tool which consists of a handle and four different sized ferrules
Hammer
Foam pad or towel to act as a cushion for the eyes or nose
Screwdriver, pliers, and wire cutters

For wiring

Pipe cleaners
No. 16 gauge galvanized wire
Adhesive tape
Wire cutters
Thin, round-nosed pliers
Heavy duty pliers for thicker wire

Patterns, Layouts, and Cutting

Accurate pattern making is essential for making toys that will fit together correctly. For making full size patterns of any toy in this book, you will need large sheets of paper marked with a squared grid. The grid scale is marked on each pattern graph and it will always be one inch. Dressmaker's pattern paper from sewing departments and graph paper from stationers come marked in 1″ squares. Or you may prefer to make your own squared paper using a ruler and a set square with a right angle. Remember that a sheet of letter paper or foolscap paper has a right angle on each corner which can be traced around.

If you intend to use a pattern several times or are cutting a toy from fur fabric, it will be necessary to make a card copy of the pattern. Card from such common sources as cereal boxes is quite adequate. These patterns can then be kept in large envelopes or be tied with a pipe cleaner passing through a hole punched in each piece.

Working on one square at a time, copy outline of pattern on to your grid. Continue in this way until you have made a complete copy. Sometimes only half of a pattern piece is given. Make a copy on folded paper and then cut out. When fold is opened, you will have a complete piece. Transfer all details like darts, eye, mouth, limb, and opening positions on to your copy. Also note the number of pieces of fabric to be cut and the direction in which they are to be cut. The grain of the fabric is indicated by an arrow on the pattern; mark this on each pattern piece. Felt has no grain, therefore the pattern pieces to be cut from felt will not have any arrows.

All the pattern pieces have a seam allowance of ¼″ (6 mm) included unless stated otherwise.

How to enlarge or reduce a pattern

Reducing or enlarging a pattern is often thought to be a daunting process, and for this reason tends not to be done. But it is truly quite simple and allows you to make families of your favourite toys. To enlarge or reduce, you change the scale of the grid on to which the pattern is being copied. For example, when enlarging, it can be increased from 1″ to 1½″ and the pattern made by following the procedure already outlined. To reduce a toy, you decrease the scale of the grid.

Perhaps you are worried about working out the finished size. Certainly be careful when varying the scale of a toy, for such alterations can produce quite dramatic changes in the bulk of the finished article. A linear increase of 100% will need four times as much material and will result in a toy eight times as big in bulk. Commence with small changes, say in the order of ¼″ (6 mm) in either direction.

Pattern layouts and cutting

The minimum amount of material needed to make each toy is listed and in some cases there will be only one way to lay the pattern that fits in all the pieces. It is a case of being economical with more expensive fabrics, and for this reason, some pattern layouts are included.

If no pattern layout is given, then follow the general rules of layout for fabrics without nap and for fabrics with nap. For the former, lay the pieces on the fabric with the arrows running parallel to the selvedge. For fabrics with nap, such as fur, velvet and needlecords, first find the direction of the pile by stroking. Mark this on the wrong side of the fabric by drawing a large arrow with tailor's chalk. Now lay pieces of pattern on back of fabric with all arrows running in the same direction. With velvet, the pile should go upwards for a rich effect. When making fur toys, the pattern pieces are arranged so that the direction of the pile follows that found in nature, that is, away from the nose, down the limbs, and up to the tip of the ears. Felt has no grain. Arrange the pattern pieces as closely together as possible, fitting them in like a jigsaw.

When cutting a pair of anything, say a foot, remember to reverse the pattern to get a right and a left side.

Before marking and cutting, make sure that all creases in your fabric are ironed out. Wash towelling fabric before cutting. Lay pattern pieces on wrong side of fabric, which may be doubled or single depending on the type of material you are using. Never cut through double layers of a fabric with nap. Place patterns on fold where indicated. When using fabrics with a pronounced pattern, try to position pieces carefully to make them match.

Pin pattern pieces round edges on lightweight fabrics, while on heavyweight fabrics, like fur, draw round pattern pieces using either a soft pencil or tailor's chalk. Never use pins on fur fabric as they constrict the pattern, making it smaller; just as important, from the safety point of view, they can too easily be lost in the pile. When cutting fur, move the scissors carefully between the pile, taking care to cut only the backing.

Stitching

The seams of a toy, whether worked by hand or machine, must withstand the pressure of firm stuffing. When tails, limbs, ears, and eyes are sewn on to the surface of a finished toy, they need to be secure against tugging by little fingers. Wherever possible, a sewing machine has been used for stitching, and therefore a seam allowance of $\frac{1}{4}$" (6 mm) has been allowed on the pattern pieces, unless otherwise stated. Nevertheless, small toys and dolls' clothes are often awkward to work on a machine and in this case, hand stitching with a firm backstitch is called for.

If you are making your very first toys, then it is advisable first to tack all the pieces together to achieve a good fit before finally sewing. Tacking or basting is only specifically mentioned when it is particularly necessary. This will usually be the case when a long gusset is being inserted or when two pieces of fabric need easing together. Use a running stitch to tack lightweight fabrics together and a long, oversewing stitch for fur fabrics. Tuck the pile in on the fur fabric and leave the tacking stitches in as additional strength for the seams.

You should at all times make sure that your chosen material is firm enough for the toy you are making and that the seams will hold. Materials which fray easily or are very lightweight will need special care. Allowing wider seams is one way to cope with fraying materials, and a zig zag stitch is useful for finishing all raw edges of the seams. Very lightweight fabrics can be used satisfactorily if first attached to a cotton lining, or to some iron-on

backing. If you have any doubts about the strength of a seam then work a second row of stitching or even stay stitching in particular areas.

Make sure that the needle and thread used in your machine match the fabric you are using (see table page 14).

A $\frac{1}{4}$" (6 mm) seam does not generally require any trimming along straight edges or gentle curves. However, tight curves should be trimmed narrower, parallel to the seam, not at right angles to it as this could well break the stitching. Sharp corners will need clipping to ease the tension. Use an iron to press seams wherever necessary, for example, on clothes.

Ladder stitch is a hand worked stitch essential for well made toys. It is used for closing the toy after stuffing, attaching limbs, heads, ears and all those little extras that help to create the character of a toy. To work ladder stitch, use a double length of very strong linen button thread. Make a small running stitch alternately on one side of the opening and then on the other (see Figure 1, below). After making a few stitches, pull on the thread. You will see that the ladder stitch laces up the opening, automatically turning in the raw edges and leaving a smooth join with no

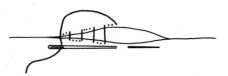

Figure 1 Ladder stitch

Fabric	Thread	Machine Needle
Lightweight fabrics such as cotton, shirting, silk, sheer woollens	Mercerized cotton No. 60–70	11
Mediumweight fabrics such as flannel, jersey, velveteen, denim, felt	No. 40–60	14
Heavyweight fabrics such as coatings, fur fabric, upholstery fabrics	No. 40	16

external signs of the thread. The advantages should be obvious. No threads for little fingers to get at, no threads on the surface to become worn, and lastly but not least, the stitches lie with the grain of the fabric, rather than pulling against it. Use it at all times, in preference to any other stitch, to attach limbs, tails, and ears.

Stab stitch is used to hold together layers of firm or thick material absolutely securely. It has the appearance of small close-together running stitches. The needle is pushed straight down through the layers vertically, and is then brought up again in the same way. The stitches should be kept very small and neat.

Stuffing

Fillings and stuffings are really a matter of individual choice and availability. They should be suitable both for the toy and the future owner. Lightweight, hygienic, fire resistant, and washable stuffings are usually demanded by the public for commercially sold toys. Indeed, there are numerous varieties covering many features of soft toys.

Kapok and foam chips are widely available, being sold by a variety of national chain stores. I find both of them awkward and messy to work with. Kapok gets everywhere, up your nose and in your clothes, and the foam chips have a habit of sticking to anything but the toy. If you use either of them, work with your hands in the bottom of a deep bag. Apart from this disadvantage, kapok is ideal for producing a really firm shape to the toy. Tiny amounts can be worked right into awkward corners and the whole toy can be properly moulded. It is also cream coloured, which makes it useful for toys where a dark stuffing would show through

the fabric skin. Remember, kapok is not washable, as it goes lumpy. Foam chips are lumpy and cannot be packed firmly together to give a smooth outline. They are best used in fur toys where a lightweight, washable filling, rather than a firm stuffing, is required. Foam chips can also be used as bulk filling in the centre of large toys like Humpty Dumpty. The chips are surrounded by any of the firmer stuffings.

Other suitable stuffings are cotton flock, Dacron, wadding, polypropylene, and Terylene. There are also industrial wastes that wash well and are fire resistant, but these are only available from a limited number of sources. Bean bags must have a flexible filling, and any of the following is suitable: rice, beans, lentils, dried peas, or millet. However, these substances are not suitable for the large floppy floor cushions that are at present popular. In this case you will need foam granules, sold under the name of Polybeads. These are fun to prepare as you have to cook or rather steam them first. The granules then expand to 60 times their original volume.

The technique of stuffing a soft toy

The technique of stuffing consists of the bulking out of the skin of a toy. Having spent time sewing a toy together, it is a mistake to rush ahead at this stage, as the only way to correct a badly stuffed toy is to empty it out and start all over again. Therefore commence by preparing the stuffing material (except foam chips), teasing it into small, fluffed up portions. These portions are pushed, one at a time, into the furthermost extremities of the skin, like feet, nose, head, hands and tail. Pack them in firmly, ramming them home with a stuffing stick. Work consistently and carefully. Mould the toy as you stuff it, making sure that there are no unfilled corners or lumps. Work back towards the opening, continually checking the firmness of the toy. Do this by trying to push your fingers into the stuffing. If you are able to make any holes, then further work is required.

At this stage, I always like to leave a large toy for several hours, as it allows the stuffing to settle and further gaps to appear, which can then be filled with extra stuffing. Finally close the toy with ladder stitch.

It is no exaggeration to say that the success of a toy depends on this stage, for without sufficient stuffing, heads flop, limbs wobble, joints will not work, clothes will not fit, and the appearance is generally poor. In addition, the life of the toy will be shorter, for it is no longer so appealing or durable.

Design and Designing

Design is the total concept of an idea. It starts with an inspiration or observation and takes shape as you work through all the stages of researching, choosing materials, selecting colour and texture of fabrics, assembly, stuffing, and the addition of character-making features. Above all, the design should be related to the future owner of a toy. This will obviously determine whether the toy is to be wired, jointed, large, small, or washable. These are some notes to help you start developing the pattern ideas given in the book as well as ideas of your own.

The objective of toy designing is to produce a stylized form that is both recognizable and attractive. If realism is required then the materials and techniques will impose limitations, for there are more suitable media in which to undertake such an exercise. Often, the simpler the shape, the greater will be the appeal of the toy. It certainly increases play possibility, because the child is given scope to use his imagination and develop a personal relationship with the toy. You have only to think of the many natural objects that are used for play, as did early designers who used socks, pegs, and shoes to create simple effects.

Where your ideas come from will largely depend on your method of working. You may see a particularly appealing antic in a young playing animal, or your children may like an animal in a book, on holiday, on the television, or at the zoo and immediately demand their own personal copy. These are the hardest of all requests to satisfy, as only one person knows exactly what he or she wants. Designers may have the same inspiration but they will rarely produce a similar result.

My training was as a professional zoologist and this totally dominates the way I look at animals and the way I work. Having had a request or inspiration for a particular toy, I need to know something about it. This may involve looking at a photograph, or become a lengthier process if the animal is not such a familiar one. While it is important to think of animals in terms of size, proportions, functional anatomy, and behaviour, for the purpose of designing a toy it is more necessary to recognize and concentrate on those features that distinguish it. For example, one can easily make a toy bird, but give it a red breast and immediately you have a robin. In this case the colour is the distinguishing feature, and it is interesting to realize that this is how robins also recognize one another. Thus every type of animal is unique, even if only in a small way. These are the features that you must incorporate in the final toy, for they will be used to identify it.

Not all animals use colour as the basis for recognition; pattern may also be important. For instance, the outline of a horse quickly becomes a zebra if black and white stripes are added. The different types of zebra are determined by thickness of stripe and positioning on body. However, these are not important in toymaking once the basic effect has been achieved. Nevertheless, the larger cats have very different patterns and shapes of marking which are worth incorporating in toys; stripes for tigers, spots for cheetahs, squarish patterns for jaguars, and manes for lions (see Figure 2, below). If there were no spots on the ladybird bean bag it would be a simple beetle. Moreover, the hippopotamus body pattern could be used for any standing animal, for the identification of the toy depends on the shape of the head.

Having determined the identifying features for your toy, decide what posture it is going to have and draw an outline shape. Is it to be a standing, sitting or lying down toy? If it is to be standing, will the legs support the weight of the body and at the same time withstand play? Whatever posture you choose, make sure that the toy is balanced and not liable to fall over. In other words, you must design the toy so that the bulk is evenly spread around a point which is the centre of gravity. Do not make the front too heavy by giving it a large, projecting head.

Now work out where you need gussets and darts. Gussets generally provide width and depth over large areas, while darts provide localized shaping. A balance of the two is a matter of experience, gained from observation plus trial and error. Unfortunately, toys have to be made and stuffed before you can see all the mistakes, although some idea of the shape may be had from pinning the pattern together and imagining it stuffed.

The simplest gusset is an even width strip inserted between a pair of identical outline shapes. Figure 2 illustrates this point. The next step is to vary the width of the gusset so

Figure 2 Simple profile, rabbit and cats

16

that it is wider over the haunches, crown of head, and tummy, and narrower at the nose and neck. As the shape of the gusset becomes more complex, it also becomes too unwieldy to work as a simple strip. Until now the toys will have been simple profile shapes, but split the gusset into various separate pieces and you have really launched yourself into pattern making.

The addition of eyes helps to secure an emotional response to your toy. Their position influences the proportions of the toy's head and therefore whether it is to be adult or young and even intelligent or foolish. The shape and style of the eye can make it sad, happy, or even provide the recognition feature, as in cats (see Figure 2). They are often put on a toy in a humanized way to provide an ensured appeal.

Therefore, when designing a toy, think of your design under the following headings:—

suitability of toy for future owner
identifying characteristics
fabrics for colour, design, and texture
outline shape of posture
character-making features
centre of gravity
gussets for bulk
darts for localized shaping

2 Toymaking Techniques

There are just a few techniques peculiar to the craft of making soft toys and dolls. These include jointing, wiring, and the insertion of glass and plastic eyes and noses. Adding musical units, chimes, growlers and squeakers demands very little skill, but is included here for the sake of convenience. The method of inserting eyes and noses is considered in Chapter Three.

Jointing

Adding joints to soft toys greatly increases their flexibility and versatility. Children do enjoy the simplest unjointed toys, but animals and dolls that move and bend can be even more fun to play with. Though it does take a little time and practice to learn the jointing technique, it is much easier than people think. After reading the following instructions, practise inserting a joint in two pieces of material before trying to make a jointed toy. After that you should be able to joint any toy with ease.

The sets of joints commonly available are made either from hardboard or wood. Each type consists of either two wooden discs or two hardboard discs each with a central clearance hole, a split cotter pin, and two steel washers (see Figure 3, opposite). The joint sets are sold in various sizes ranging from $\frac{3}{4}''$ joints for tiny limbs and heads to $6''$ joints for making the moveable heads of very large toys.

If you should need smaller joints for miniature toys then remember that snap fasteners can make a very satisfactory substitute.

In addition to the joints you will need a pair of thin, round-nosed pliers (about $\frac{1}{8}''$ across the nose) for tightening and twisting the cotter pins to the correct angle. You will also need two circles of felt, leather, or scrap fur fabric for making shields, which should be cut larger than the joint discs. They help to mask and

conceal the joint from the outside of the toy and to reduce wear and tear on the fabric of the limb resulting from the friction of the moving joint (see Figure 4, opposite). Always use the largest joints possible to fit into the jointing position. (See mail order sources, page 8).

Technique of limb jointing

The technique of jointing is presented in a series of easy to follow stages. Remember the method for all limbs, whether arms or legs, is similar.

Start by making the limb.

1 Place both limb pieces together with right sides facing and machine around edge leaving the top, that is the hip or shoulder, end open.

2 Turn limb right side out and stuff nearly to the top.

3 Pierce the position of the joint with a knitting needle to make a hole for the cotter pin. This position is marked on the pattern.

4 Take the split cotter and, holding the eye between your fingers, thread on to the tail end a steel washer, disc, and a fabric shield, in that order.

5 Now push cotter tail through the joint position marked by the hole in stage 3 (see Figure 5A, page 20).

18

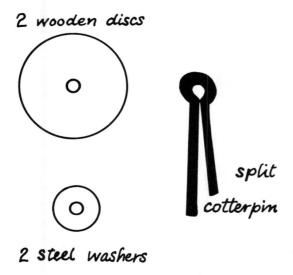

2 wooden discs

split cotterpin

2 steel washers

Figure 3 A typical joint set

6 Insert more stuffing around joint and close the shoulder or hip opening with ladder stitch (see Figure 5B, page 20).

7 The limb is now ready for jointing to the body (see Figure 5C, page 20).

8 With a knitting needle, make a hole in the wall of the body at the joint position, which is marked on the pattern.

9 Push tail end of cotter, projecting from the limb, through this hole.

10 Thread on to the cotter tail a fabric shield, wooden disc, and a steel washer.

11 Now lay the toy on a table so that the limb is against the table and the body is uppermost. Hold the disc firmly between your fingers, pressing down on to the table. Alternatively you may prefer to pinch the pieces of the joint in the body and limb between your fingers and thumb.

12 Split arms of the cotter pin apart and take one arm of the tail between your pliers. Then at the same time as you pull it up firmly, turn the arm over and bend it down to turn sharply against the disc (see Figure 5D, page 20).

13 Pull and turn the other arm of the tail in the same way.

The pull on the cotter must be maintained while you are turning the tail down. This draws all the pieces of the joint tightly together whilst the turning locks it into position. If you follow these stages carefully, you will make really firm joints that will last indefinitely. This is most important, because joints have a natural tendency to work loose over a long period of time. If you are not entirely happy with the joint this is probably because the pieces are not locked together tightly enough. Therefore recommence by straightening the cotter pin and remaking the joint. Occasionally a weak cotter pin will snap with the additional bending and unbending. For this reason it is advisable to keep spare cotters, which are obtainable from hardware merchants.

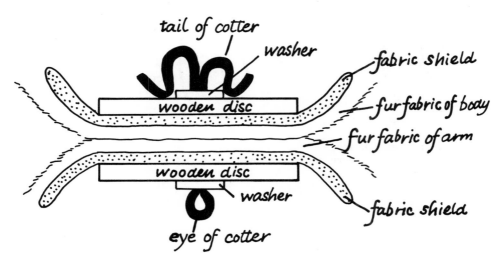

tail of cotter

washer

fabric shield

wooden disc

fur fabric of body

fur fabric of arm

wooden disc

washer

fabric shield

eye of cotter

Figure 4 Cross section of joint in position

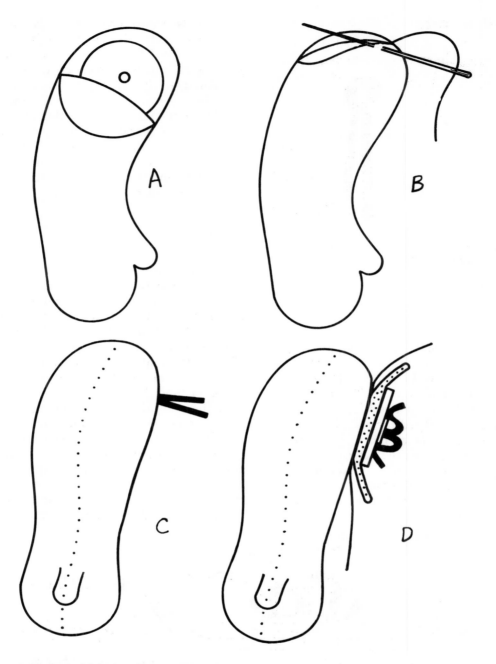

Figure 5 Method of jointing an arm
A. Position of joint in arm   B. Arm being closed with ladder stitch   C. Arm ready for jointing to body
D. Arm jointed to body

Alternative technique of limb jointing

A jointed toy should have rounded shoulders and hips that completely mask the presence of any joints. If it is difficult to achieve this by the method described, try the following alternative method. This is particularly useful when working with very small joints.

1 Work through stages 1, 2, and 3 of the previous method for jointing a limb.
2 Take the split cotter and holding the eye between your fingers thread on a steel washer, disc, large circle of cotton material, and a fabric shield.
3 Push tail end of cotter through the joint position in wall of limb.
4 Run a gathering thread around the edge of the cotton circle and pull up to form a cup. Place a ball of stuffing in this cup and finish pulling on the gathering thread. Fasten off. You will now have enclosed the joint in a bag of stuffing and thereby completely masked it from the outside of the toy (see Figure 6, below).
5 Finish stuffing the limb and close the opening with ladder stitch.
6 Proceed from stage 8 onwards of the previous method, deciding whether or not it is necessary to repeat this operation and make another cotton bag to cover the joint in the body.

Technique of jointing a head

There are no patterns given for a toy with a jointed head in this book, but by following either of the methods described below you should be able to insert a joint in the neck of any suitable toy. The most important point to remember is that a head joint should be as wide as the neck to reduce the chance of a future wobble. For this reason the largest available joints will be used. You must therefore adapt the patterns for any toy in which you wish to insert a head joint. This means that the neck edge of both the head and body pieces must be extended.

Method One

This is the simplest method.

1 Add on at least one inch to the neck edge of both head and body when cutting from fabric. This extra material will be gathered up to cover the joint. The disadvantage is that the gathers form a bulk between the discs which prevents a really tight joint being formed.
2 Prepare the head so that it is stuffed tightly down to the neck and is ready for jointing.
3 Run a gathering thread around the raw edge of the neck.

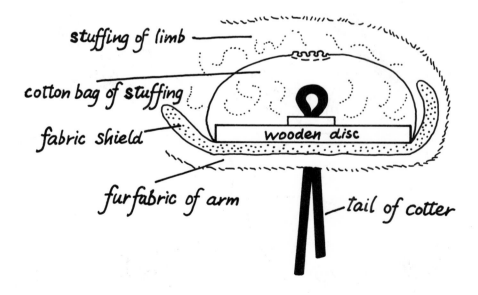

stuffing of limb

cotton bag of stuffing

fabric shield

wooden disc

fur fabric of arm

tail of cotter

Figure 6 Cross section of joint with additional stuffing

21

4 Thread a steel washer and disc on to the cotter pin.

5 Place the prepared joint in neck with tail of cotter projecting outwards (see Figure 7A, below).

6 Pull up the gathering thread so that the joint is completely enclosed in the head.

7 Work a series of criss cross stitches over the neck opening to hold all excess material down flat against the joint. Put head aside (see Figure 7B, below).

8 Make the skin of the body and turn right side out, remembering to leave an opening other than the neck for stuffing. Run a gathering thread around the neck edge, pull up tightly and fasten off securely.

9 Now take up the head and gently push tail end of cotter between stitching at neck of body. Be careful that no stitches pass between the split pin as the movement of the head during playing could break the stitches and result in the neck coming apart.

10 Thread fabric shield, disc, and steel washer in that order on to tail of cotter.

11 Now complete the jointing by pulling on each of the cotter arms, and turning into a locked position.

Method Two

This method is more involved, but is well worth the effort. The bulk of gathers between the discs is completely removed so that the discs on each side of the neck lie close together.

1 Prepare the head so that it is stuffed firmly down to the neck.

2 Select a joint that is just slightly smaller than the neck opening, say by half an inch.

3 Cut two circles of the fabric used for making the toy, about half an inch larger all round than the disc. One will be used as a shield for the joint while the other will form an outside covering that will eventually be stitched to the head.

4 Lay fabric circles together with a right side to a wrong side and run a gathering thread around the edge. Place disc in the centre of the fabric on the wrong side and pull up tightly on gathering thread. Fasten off.

5 Push a knitting needle through centre of disc to make a hole in the fabric.

6 Thread a steel washer on to the cotter pin and then push tail end through clearance hole on the uncovered side of disc (see Figure 8, opposite).

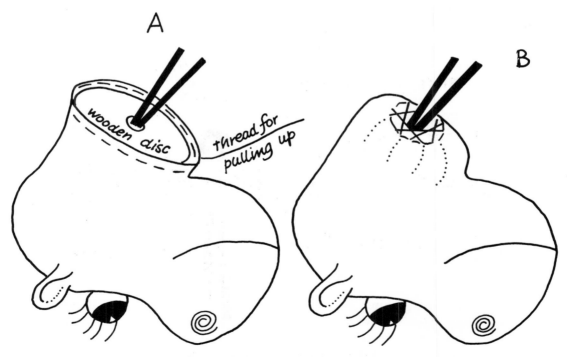

Figure 7 First method of preparing head for jointing
A. Joint inserted in open neck   B. Neck opening closed around joint

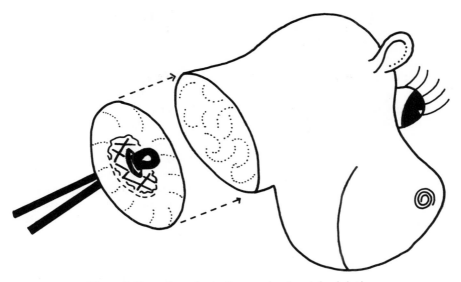

Figure 8 Second method of preparing head for jointing

7 Place the prepared joint against the neck opening of head with cotter eye lying inwards amongst the stuffing. Ladder stitch joint to neck edge, working in additional stuffing that will be needed and turning in the raw edges of the neck as you work.

8 Make up a body skin. Cut a circle of fabric just larger than the disc and sew this to the neck opening – easing edges so that they fit evenly together. Pierce the centre of the neck circle with a knitting needle. Turn skin right side out.

9 Take up the head and push the tail end of the cotter through hole in the neck circle of the body.

10 Thread on to the cotter tail a fabric shield, disc, and steel washer.

11 Complete the jointing by pulling on each of the cotter arms and turning to lock.

Patterns for jointed toys are rather limited, both in number and scope. They tend to be confined to traditional teddy bears and rabbits. An enterprising toymaker will soon design her own patterns, incorporating joints for such features as movable tails, wings, eyes, waists, and feelers, to name but a few of the more obvious examples. What about a caterpillar with jointed segments? It would need to be little more than a chain of furry balls jointed to each other.

Wiring

Traditionally, wiring was used for strengthening soft toys and for maintaining a characteristic posture. It was unquestionably put into the more realistic toys of our predecessors.

Now there is a tendency to stylize toys to a more simple and basic shape that does not require wiring. I personally prefer this approach and design toys for young children in such a way that the question 'whether to wire or not', never arises. For wires must be regarded as a potential source of danger for young children.

Nevertheless, this technique must not be totally ignored, as it can be used quite safely in the realistic and ornamental toys so popular with older children. These toys are really objects to be looked at and admired for their design rather than to be played with.

Toys with a wired skeleton can be made in two different ways, depending on their size. There is a method used for small toys with thin legs. Here the wire is bent into the appropriate shape and the fabric skin sewn around it, on the outside. These toys are nearly always made from felt because there are no problems of turning in raw edges. The other method is for larger toys where there is plenty of space around the skeleton for inserting stuffing. Here the fabric skin is sewn on the wrong side, turned right side out, and stuffing plus skeleton inserted. Thus the wire skeleton is embedded in a cushion of stuffing.

Technique for preparing a wire skeleton

The length of wire needed for the skeleton is estimated by measuring the distance down each leg, along back of body and up neck or whatever part is being wired. This length is then doubled and cut. Bend wire into shape, turning it back on itself to give a double framework.

Make sure that the two cut ends lie in the middle along the back and not in a leg (see Figure 9, below). Twist the wires together. For example, hold with the pliers the two wires at the top of a leg, then place a nail in the loop at the bottom and using this as a key wind the two wires together.

Bind the wires with adhesive tape (pink medical or electrical), paying particular attention to the cut ends. Roll stuffing over the covered wire and hold in place with thread or wool. The amount of stuffing used depends on how thick you want the skeleton to be. A wired skeleton need not be of uniform thickness.

Now take a length of seam tape or even strips of rag and bind around stuffing, completely enclosing it. Using slip stitch, catch the edges together at intervals (see Figure 10, opposite). Foam sheeting or strips of foam may be used to wrap around the wires, replacing the stuffing and tape.

Often a complete skeleton like the one described is unnecessary and a simple 'U' shaped bridge between each pair of fore legs or hind legs will provide sufficient strength for a standing toy. In this instance, the legs hold the body off the ground, allowing the toy to stand firmly in a characteristic posture.

Wires for other purposes

Sometimes certain features of a toy, other than the main skeleton, may need individual strengthening. Examples are the legs and necks of some birds, antlers and horns of mammals, tentacles of snails, legs and wings of insects, feelers and legs of crabs and lobsters, tusks of walruses, elephants, and dinosaurs, and even teeth and claws of many animals.

In many instances pipe cleaners can be used in these situations. They come ready prepared, cushioned in their own stuffing, and you will

Figure 9 Sketch of Woolly Mammoth showing skeletal wire in position. The tusks have a separate wire skeleton.

find them used for the legs of the spider in this book. Remember too that thick fuse wire, millinery wire, and even florist's wire could all have their uses in wiring toys. No hard and fast rules can be laid down; it is up to you to experiment and see what is best suited to your design.

Dowel rods

The use of dowel rods is advocated for strengthening the necks of dolls, clowns, and long-necked animals, where no flexibility or subsequent bending is required. It is even possible to combine dowelling and wires.

Musical Units and Toy Voices

Amongst the more expensive toys presently on sale are the talking dolls with a repertoire of several sentences, and musical plush animals. However, the simpler sounds produced by growlers, squeakers and chimes are inexpensive and very easy to incorporate into many toys. Endless hours of play can be had from turning teddy backwards and forwards to listen for his growl, rolling him over and over to hear his chime, or pressing his tummy to make him squeak.

Musical units have a special charm of their own. So many different tunes are available, from favourite nursery rhymes and lullabies to current hit parade melodies. Apart from the cost, there is no problem in including them in a toy. A simple toy can thus be transformed into a luxury gift suitable for a very special occasion. (See mail order sources, page 8).

Growlers and squeakers

These voices are considered together as they have a similar method of insertion. They are both plastic cylinders containing bellows. The growler has the deeper voice of the two, and being larger, it is suitable for a big toy. One end of the growler has a series of holes and these must lie next to the fabric skin of the body. The noise from a squeaker is produced by a reed lying at one end of the narrow cylinder. Thus it is suitable for inclusion in small toys, designed for young children. The reed must always be placed against the fabric skin.

It is necessary to anchor these units to the fabric skin of the toy. Usually the cylinder is enclosed in a tight fitting bag which can be made from an open mesh cotton or similar material. However, with care, it is possible to

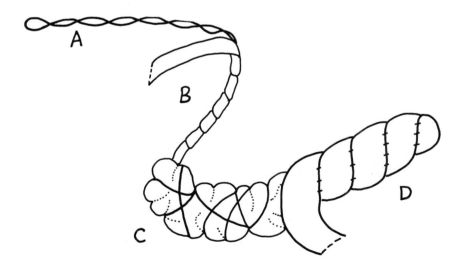

Figure 10 Preparation of wire
A. Cut end of wire turned back and twisted against main shaft   B. Adhesive tape bound over wires
C. Cushion of stuffing held in place with thread   D. Tape wound over stuffing and stitched in place

stick a cloth strip with a projecting collar around the unit; use a latex glue. Place the unit in the toy through the centre back opening. Lay it amongst the stuffing with the reed or holes next to the body wall. Stitch in place to toy skin through fabric bag or collar with tiny, almost invisible, stitches. Finish stuffing the toy and close the centre back seam. Some modern squeakers are waterproof and the toy is therefore washable, but do check this when buying the unit.

Chimes

These voices are also known as 'tinkle bells' or just 'tinklers'. A chime is a plastic cylinder which produces the noise when it is shaken or rolled. The rolling allows a weight to pass over steel pins of different lengths and so make a tinkle. The cylinder is completely closed so that it is waterproof and the toy itself becomes washable. Some older types of chimes and tinklers are still made from cardboard and these are definitely *not* waterproof.

Chimes can be put inside toys with large tummies. They do not have to be stitched or anchored in any special way – just embed them firmly amongst the stuffing. The scholar, Aristotle, on Page 39, could be made around a chime instead of the cardboard cylinder.

Musical units

Care must be taken when selecting a toy suitable for inserting a musical unit, for the latter is comparatively large and heavy. If positioned incorrectly the toy can become rather clumsy because the centre of gravity will be in an awkward position. For this reason, sitting or reclining toys are eminently suitable.

The units are enclosed in a plastic shell which protects the delicate movement from the surrounding stuffing. However, they are *not* waterproof, so the toys can only be surface cleaned. The movement is wound either by a key or a pull string. The pull string is drawn out to start the tune and slowly moves back towards the toy. Think of a novel way to make use of this string. Sew a ball around it so that as the tune plays, the ball moves towards a dog. Sew a spider to the end and have it move towards Miss Muffet. The unit is inserted in a partially stuffed toy with the key projecting through either a hole pierced for the purpose or the stuffing opening. Finish stuffing and close the opening.

3 Character-Making Features

The identity of a toy is primarily determined by the design of the pattern. This is further highlighted by the choice of fabric and any other feature peculiar to that animal, say for instance, the mane of a lion. However, the type of mane also helps to create or change the character. For example, a lion with a large, thick mane in a rich yellow or black is a proud, bold, aggressive animal while a thin, dirty coloured, mangy mane would be found on a sad, old lion. Thus the mane establishes the identity and has additional value in giving character. In contrast the colour and shape of the eyes provide the identity, while variation in the position determines the character, giving an intelligent or stupid-looking animal. I am emphasizing here the emotional features which create the character of the animal. You will soon learn that there is a narrow dividing line between a toy that looks right and one that looks wrong. It may be a very subtle difference of relationship of features to one another, so keep moving them around until you have the desired character.

Eyes

Expressions of sadness, happiness, friendliness, pensiveness, and cheekiness are largely determined by the type, size and position of the eyes. These emotional features contribute enormously to the success and appeal of a toy; therefore, take great care when adding them.

The only satisfactory way to determine the position of eyes is to closely observe the animal that you are making as a toy. Look at it in real life or refer to photographs. Is the animal a hunter with eyes directed forward? Is the animal swift of foot with eyes directed sideways? Is the animal one that lives on land and in the water and has raised eyes, like crocodiles, hippopotamuses, and frogs? Does the animal hunt by night and have very large eyes? Ask yourself all these questions, and when you are satisfied with the answers come back to the toy. Place the eyes in the position that you have observed is correct for that animal. Never rush this part of toymaking for the sake of a quickly finished article.

Youthfulness can be indicated by positioning them farther apart and low down on the face. Bring them closer together and you have a mean looking individual. Place them too high on the head and the toy becomes senseless. There are various reasons to explain why these things happen; for example, if the eyes are too high, then there can be no room for the brain. As well as positioning the eye, do not forget to arrange the individual parts of the eye, like the pupil, to capture the required expression. Wrongly placed, the toy could be vacant or even cross-eyed.

There are many types of eye to choose from. Commercially produced eyes include glass and plastic eyes on wire, plastic safety lock in eyes, and joggle eyes. Beads, sequins, and buttons can all be used, either on their own or with felt and embroidery. The last two offer an opportunity to make distinctive eyes beyond the scope of plastic and glass eyes.

Glass eyes

These eyes are usually sold in pairs, connected by a length of wire. They range in size from 6 mm to 24 mm and come in a variety of colours and styles. There are the common brown, blue, and green eyes and then the more unusual rabbit eye with red pupil, cat eye with slit pupil, and dog eye with white corner.

Separate the eyes by cutting the wire $\frac{3}{4}''$ (2 cm) from each eye. Make a shank by turning the wire into a narrow loop with thin-nosed pliers. Make sure that the end of the wire is tightly wrapped around the base of the shank and that a thread could not break loose from the loop. Thread a double length of very strong linen thread or even fine string through the loop. Now tie the eye in the middle of the threads with a slip knot. Make a hole in the face fabric in the eye position. Do this with a steel knitting needle.

Thread one set of double threads on to a long darning needle and pass it through the head to the other side. Repeat this stage with the remaining double thread. For forward facing eyes, the threads can be passed either to the nape of the neck or across the face to emerge under the ear on the opposite side of the head (see Figures 11A and 11B, below). The threads that pass to the neck are tied off together in a reef knot, then each end is darned in and 'lost' in the head, well away from the

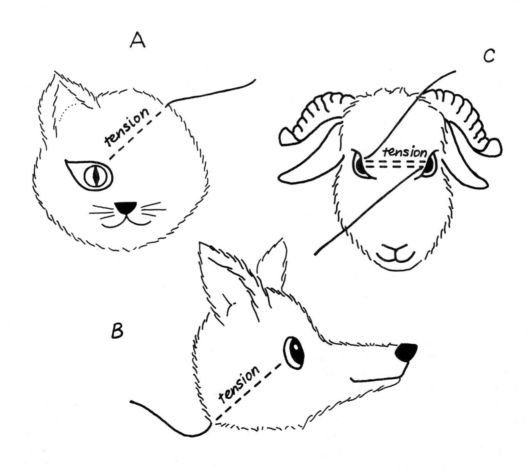

Figure 11 Method of inserting glass eyes
A. Forward facing eyes tied off at ears   B. Forward facing eyes tied off at neck   C. Sideways facing eyes tied off behind each other

knot. Threads that emerge by the ears are also knotted and the ends darned in, independently of each other, before being cut.

For sideways facing animals, the threads are passed across the face to emerge on the opposite side by the eye. They are then tied off behind each eye and stitched away before being cut (see Figure 11C, page 28).

No matter which direction the threads take, always pull on them very tightly when fastening off. The shank must pass through the hole in the face fabric and leave only the eye on the surface. The tension on the thread will also form a socket around the eye, thus providing additional shaping to the face.

Joggle (wiggle) eyes

These are mainly white eyes with a clear front and a moving pupil. Some are made like a button so that you sew them on to the toy while others have a shank and are fixed on with a safety washer.

Safety lock in eyes

These eyes range in size from 6 mm to 24 mm. Colours are similar to those of glass eyes and again there are eyes designed specifically for cats, with a slit pupil. A special fixing tool is needed to insert these eyes. It consists of a handle and four separate magnetized ferrules. Each eye has a shank, and the correct sized ferrule for that eye locks the safety washer on to the shank with the face fabric firmly wedged between the two. Once a safety lock in eye is inserted, it is quite impossible to remove, so you must be sure of its position before you proceed.

Take the finished skin of a toy and place some stuffing in the head only. Press the eyes against the fabric, making sure that they are level with each other and equally spaced. The shanks will momentarily leave an impression on the fabric and you can mark this position with a soft pencil. Remove the stuffing from the head.

Make a hole in the eye position, just large enough to admit the shank of the eye. Insert shank from the right side, place washer on the magnetized ferrule and then position this against the shank from the wrong side. Protect the eye by resting it on a foam pad or

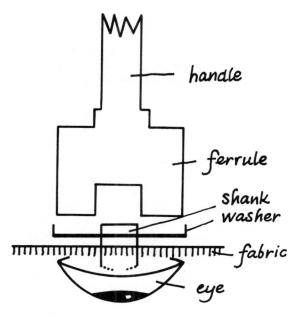

Figure 12 Safety lock in eye and fixing tool

folded hand towel. Now push the washer down on to the shank by giving the fixing tool a sharp tap with a hammer (see Figure 12, above). There should be no space between the washer, material, and eye. A careful toymaker will never take the eye position, marked on the pattern, for granted. Uneven sewing, say too large a seam or too small a seam, will quickly alter this position and thereby destroy the required character.

If by any chance you must remove an eye, then cut the washer with wire cutters and lever it off with a screwdriver. I then repair the hole by darning it and sticking a felt patch over the area on the wrong side. You may just be able to reinsert an eye through the repair but this will rather depend on your skill. Better to work a felt eye on the outside and so cover the mistake.

Fur fabrics with a knitted backing stretch too much to take these eyes without some additional preparation. Stick a large patch of felt on the wrong side, then proceed as above. (See mail order sources, page 8).

Hand made eyes

With felt eyes you can create a wide range of characters, for felt can be cut to any shape or size and the various parts can be arranged to

29

give the exact expression required. As felt is rather flat, work highlights on the pupils. Cut a small notch to expose the white of the eye, sew a small group of white satin stitches on the pupil or even sew on shiny beads and sequins in small clusters. Another way of adding a highlight is to cut a small shape of light coloured felt and stitch or glue it to the pupil. The eyes can also be raised by cutting a double white eye shape and stitching the two together, with a small amount of stuffing between the layers. With larger eyes that are stitched directly on to the face, insert the stuffing as you work. Raising the eyes is necessary when you are attaching them to a pile fabric, otherwise they tend to be lost.

Bulbous eyes can be made by gathering a circle of fabric and filling the centre with stuffing. This is the method used for the hippopotamus and Jotho, the clown.

Embroidered eyes incorporate fine detail and are more usually worked on rag dolls.

Eyelashes and eyebrows

Animals like camels, cows, and giraffes have long, expressive eyelashes. Look for them the next time you have an opportunity and you will see that they give the animal a soft, feminine expression. Therefore, when added to a toy, they can often make a fierce animal seem more friendly and cuddly. Make them from felt strips or use embroidery stitches like buttonhole stitch. Eyebrows can also be embroidered for a soft look or cut from felt and appliquéd to the face. Figure 13, opposite, will provide some ideas.

Mouths

As a general rule, mouths should indicate happiness. This can be achieved by turning up the corners to make a smile. Sadness is a downward curved mouth, meanness is a thin mouth, and a pout is a short mouth with puckered lips. Fur toys generally have the mouth outlined in mercerized cotton, while fabric toys tend to have felt outline mouths or embroidery. Instructions for making many different styles of mouth will be found throughout the book but always endeavour to experiment with ideas of your own (see Figure 14, page 32).

Dragons, sharks, and crocodiles can be made to look really ferocious by showing rows of sharp-edged teeth through an opened mouth. White ric rac or white felt are the materials commonly used for making teeth.

The position of a mouth can also be indicated by a tongue. This is especially so with puppies and kittens.

Noses

Most toys have a nose worked on the face. If it is embroidered it will likely be in conjunction with a mouth so that the two are worked together as a unit. Or it may be represented by the nostrils which need only be two french knots. Commercially prepared noses are made either from plastic or glass. Like the commercially prepared eyes, they are either wired or of the safety lock in variety. The size range is limited and the colour is restricted to black. The method used for inserting these noses is the same as that described for the eyes, so refer back for instructions.

Beads and buttons, especially the knobbly ones, can make satisfactory noses when the toy is for an older child. But the nose you make from fabric can have character all of its own. It can be an opportunity to introduce colour, as in the Harvest Mice, or to create character, as in Jotho the clown. Whatever the purpose, remember that in real life a nose is used for smelling. The nose is used for hunting food and for sensing the presence of other animals whether it be the same kind or an enemy. It should be prominent, healthy, and functional. For this reason, a nose made from black shiny material like satin is more realistic than one made from felt. Felt, however, does not fray and has been the most popular fabric for noses. See Figure 14, page 32, for ideas.

Whiskers

Whiskers are particularly characteristic of hunting animals like cats, seals, rodents, and hedgehogs. They may be worked on a toy in two ways. Firstly there are the embroidered whiskers that have both ends securely stitched into the toy. Then there are the whiskers that hang free, being attached at their base only. With either method of attachment, make sure that they are firmly anchored and that no prickly whiskers are put on to toys for very young children.

Horsehair, thin nylon fishing line, invisible sewing thread, wool, and lurex thread can all be used to make hanging whiskers. Take a length of whisker and sew securely at base of whisker position. Pass the whisker through to the other side of the face, leaving a loop on the side just worked. Sew a few catch stitches on the second side and make another loop by passing the thread back to the starting point.

Continue working in this way, anchoring in all the loops and adding new threads as required. When you have enough whisker loops, cut them and trim to shape and size wanted.

Manes

A mane is the long hair on the neck of a mammal such as a horse, lion, anteater or baboon. A healthy beast has a thick, rich mane. Manes are made on toys by fringed wool, looped curls, groups of tassels, strips of long pile fur, fringed material, fringed felt, folded and fringed felt and even plaits (braids) if for a show horse. See Figure 15, page 32, for ideas.

Figure 13 Some ideas for eyelashes and eyebrows

31

Figure 14 Some ideas for mouths and noses
A. Satin stitch and straight stitch mouths and noses   B. French knots and buttonhole stitch   C: Felt shapes   D. Pompom   E. Stuffed ball

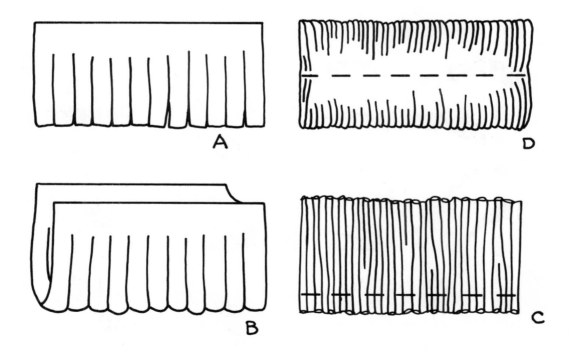

Figure 15 Some ideas for manes
A. Fringed felt   B. Looped felt   C. Fringed wool   D. Looped wool
Figure 16 Cheeks and freckles

1 Designing with Circles (opposite)
Top, from left to right: guinea pig, spider, ducks. *Middle:* panda, snail, guinea pig. *Bottom:* octopus, millipede.

Cheeks and Freckles

Both character and colour are provided by cheeks and freckles when they are worked on the rather colourless fabrics used for making rag dolls. Cheeks are regarded as a feminine character while freckles tend to indicate masculinity, hence they are found on girl and boy dolls respectively.

Freckles need be no more than a small cluster of biscuit coloured french knots. Cheeks add a warm glow to the face of a doll. Coloured felt

circles can be used on large dolls but are better left off a small doll as they tend to be too heavy and distract from the more important features. Use white felt instead and sew it in place with three strands of pink embroidery cotton.

Cheeks can also be made by working a circular patch of running stitch. Pack the stitches close together in the centre and farther apart towards the edge of the cheek. Figure 16, below, shows four different ways to work cheeks.

Painted Features

Recent developments with fabric dyes have produced several methods whereby you can decorate plain fabric with your own design. This is invaluable for making the characteristic stripes and spots of cats, stripes of zebras, and any other pattern which is a distinguishing feature. Likewise, it is also possible to mark facial features on rag dolls.

The features may be painted directly on to cloth by using a mixture of Dylon Paintex and Dylon Cold Dye. The Paintex thickens the dye so that it can be used with a brush. It is suitable for cotton, linen, silk, and soft leathers. Full instructions for fixing the dye are provided with the Paintex.

Another liquid dye paint is Rowney Fabric Printing Dye. This can also be applied with a brush and is suitable for use on cottons, linens, and some synthetic fabrics. However, the method of fixing the dye is different to that of the Paintex. You will find the instructions with the dye when you buy it.

You may prefer to draw the features with Finart Fabricrayons. The crayon has a dye incorporated in it. The features are drawn first on to paper which is then laid face down on to the fabric. A warm iron passed over the layers transfers all the details to the fabric and at the same time fixes the dye. This is a very clean technique and so is suitable for children. Let them decorate their own dollies. Crayon dyes are for use on synthetic fabrics like orlon, crimplene, and vilene. Exact details are provided with the crayons.

Apart from painting features on to dolls and making distinguishing body patterns, the dyes can also be used to decorate clothes with small personal motifs. The dyes can also be mixed to produce an infinite variety of colours, many of which could not be bought, no matter how hard you searched.

Other paints such as Flo-Paque and Jet-Pak Sprayon are available by mail. (See mail order sources, page 8).

Figure 16 Cheeks and freckles

2 The Scholars (opposite)
From top, moving clockwise: Socrates, Aristotle and pupils, Copernicus, Hippocrates, Plato.

4　Designing with Circles

All of these toys have been made from circles of non-fraying material. With these you can very quickly produce simple, yet effective results. If you intend making a number of these objects, or experimenting with your own designs, commence by preparing a series of card templates with diameters ranging between 2″ (5 cm) and 8″ (20 cm). Each circle of material is prepared by running a gathering thread around the edge. Some are then stuffed to form a ball, as in the guinea pig, whilst others are used, in floppy toys, unstuffed and pressed flat to form discs. An example of the latter is the millipede. The discs of material are threaded together on elastic cord. Children quickly realize the play potential of pulling them apart and letting them spring back into position. Imagine the toy made on a large scale – about four feet long.

Guinea Pig

The domestic guinea pig so frequently kept by children as a pet is derived from the Peruvian cavy.

Materials: a 5″ (12.5 cm) circle of fur
small amount of stuffing
small piece of felt for base and ears
2 small beads for eyes

Cutting: Make a pattern of the base and ears from the pattern graph and then cut these pieces from the felt.

Run a gathering thread around the edge of the circle and pull it up to form a cup. Fill cup with stuffing and finish pulling up the thread to close, thus forming a ball. Fasten off securely and press between your hands to mould into an oval shape. Cover the gatherings with the felt base, which may be either glued or stitched in place. Sew the beads on to each side of the head. Fold an ear in half and catch the fold at the base with a stitch, then sew securely to the head, just above and behind an eye. Work the other ear in the same way. Finish the guinea pig by brushing and clipping away any fur from around the eyes.

Panda

Giant Pandas are found only in the more remote provinces of China, where they live in bamboo forests, feeding on the tender young leaves. They are very rare and in danger of extinction. It is for this reason that the Giant Panda has been adopted as the symbol of the World Wildlife Fund.

Materials: an 8″ (20 cm) circle of black fur
a 6″ (15 cm) circle of white fur
small amount of stuffing
black fur for ears
pair of 12 mm brown safety eyes
black felt

Cutting: Make a pattern of the ears and eye
patch from the pattern graph. Cut
the ears from black fur and the eye
patch from black felt.

Gather and stuff both fur circles as described for the guinea pig. Arrange them so that you have the white head above the black body and the gathers hidden in the neck. Ladder stitch them together. Place two ear pieces together, with right sides facing, and sew around the outer curved edge. Turn right side out and sew to the head. Make the other ear in the same way. Fasten eyes into the black felt eye patches. Sew these to the face. Work a nose in black thread. Finish the panda by grooming and tying a ribbon around the neck.

Octopus

These animals were once feared, for it was believed that they could engulf ships with their eight arms and even cause them to sink. Fortunately we know now that this is impossible.

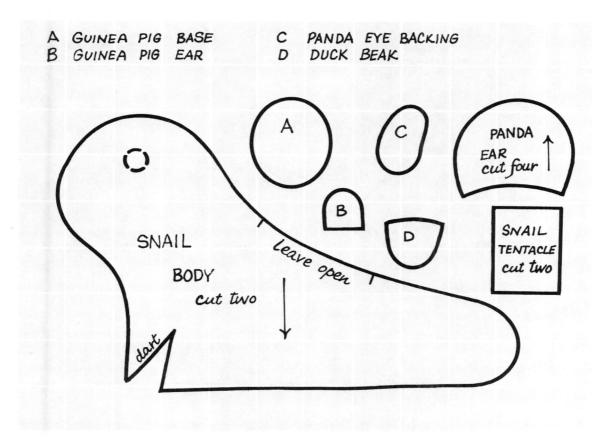

A GUINEA PIG BASE
B GUINEA PIG EAR
C PANDA EYE BACKING
D DUCK BEAK

A

C

PANDA EAR cut four

B

D

SNAIL TENTACLE cut two

SNAIL BODY cut two

Leave open

dart

Pattern graph 1 Designing with Circles *one square = 1″ (2·5cm)*

Materials: an 8″ (20 cm) circle of fur
small amount of stuffing
1 oz (28 g) double knitting wool
pair of joggle eyes
a 6″ (15 cm) circle of tartan
small amount of red wool

Gather the fur circle and lightly stuff as de-scribed for the guinea pig. Use all the wool to make four plaits (braids) of equal length. Lay these in pairs across the gatherings of the fur circle. Arrange them so that you have eight arms of equal length. Stitch securely in place. Attach the eyes.

Gather and lightly stuff the circle of tartan to make the Tam o' Shanter. Make a small tassel with the red wool and sew this to the top of the hat. Now ladder stitch the Tam o' Shanter to the octopus and slightly flatten it into the correct shape.

Duck

Our first impressions of ducks are based on the common farmyard varieties. There are, how-ever, a vast number of different types, some of which are flightless.

Materials: a 6″ (15 cm) circle of yellow fur
a 7″ (17.5 cm) circle of yellow fur
small amount of stuffing
small piece of orange felt
pair of joggle eyes
a 6″ (15 cm) circle of blue felt
a 3″ (7.5 cm) circle of foam
3″ (7.5 cm) × ½″ (13 mm) blue felt

Cutting: Make a pattern of the beak from the pattern graph and then cut from the orange felt. Graph is on page 34.

Gather and lightly stuff the two fur circles as described for the guinea pig. Arrange them to make a head and body with the gathers hidden in the neck. Sew securely together. Sew the beak together around the outer edge, stuff firmly, and sew to head.

Attach the eyes.

Make the hat by running a gathering thread around the edge of the blue felt circle. Lay the foam pad in the centre and then pull on the gathering thread. Fasten off. Fold the tab in half and sew to the side of the hat. Now ladder stitch the hat to the head of the duck. Finally, cut out a notch from both ends of the tab.

Spider

Spiders are not classified as insects, because they have four pairs of legs, whereas insects have only three pairs.

Materials: a 6″ (15 cm) circle of fabric
small amount of stuffing
a 4″ (10 cm) circle of fabric
8 pipe cleaners
felt for the legs
a 3″ (7.5 cm) circle of fabric
beads or rounded buttons for eyes

Gather and lightly stuff the largest circle to make the abdomen. The head is made by gathering and stuffing the 4″ (10 cm) circle.

Mould the head into an oval shape by pressing with your fingers as you did for the guinea pig. Place the head to the abdomen so that the head gathers are covered by the neck. Ladder stitch the two together.

The legs are made by covering pipe cleaners with felt. Cut a strip of felt the length of a pipe cleaner and just wide enough to roll around two pipe cleaners. Lay it around the pipe cleaners and close with small slip stitches.

Prepare three more legs in the same way. Now, lay all four legs across the gatherings on the underside of the abdomen so that they project equally on each side to make the eight legs of a spider. Stitch each leg securely in place. Turn under the raw edges of the smallest fabric circle and place over the leg attachment area. Hem in place.

Sew two fancy buttons or large beads in place as eyes. All that remains to be done now is to bend the legs so that the spider can stand.

Millipede

Millipedes are close relations of spiders and insects. They may be as long as 6″ (15 cm), although most are much smaller. They live amongst the leaves and twigs of woodland debris.

Materials: at least 35 circles of fabric 6″ (15 cm) in diameter
a 7″ (17.5 cm) circle of fur
small amount of stuffing
millinery elastic
2 trouser buttons
a 4″ (10 cm) circle of fabric
black and white felt for eyes
bead for nose
a 6″ (15 cm) circle of felt
a 4″ (10 cm) circle of felt

Prepare all the fabric circles for the body by gathering around the edge and fastening off. Press the circles between your fingers to form flattened discs. The more discs you make, the more exciting the millipede will be to play with. Make the head by gathering and stuffing the fur circle, but do not fasten off just yet.

Take a 24″ (61 cm) length of elastic and thread it through a trouser button. Tie a knot in the elastic so that the button is firmly lodged in the middle. Now insert the button in the opening of the head and place it amongst the stuffing. Fasten off the gatherings securely around the two projecting arms of elastic.

Pierce each fabric disc by pushing a steel knitting needle through the centre, between the gathers. Now thread the elastic through the hole you have just made in all the discs. Tie the ends of the elastic through the second trouser button. This is far more secure than just knotting the ends. Gather the single, small fabric circle and lightly stuff. Before fastening off the gatherings, place the tail end button amongst the stuffing. This makes a neat ending that hides the button.

Cut two circles each of black and white felt to make the eyes. Sew them to the face of the millipede. Use a bead or interesting knobbly button to make a nose.

Prepare the cap by gathering and lightly stuffing the large circle of felt. Sew a flat button to the crown if desired. Make the brim by cutting the smaller felt circle in half. Place the two halves together and sew around the curved edge. Turn right side out and lay the opened edge on the underside of the crown. Baste and sew in position, checking that the brim projects evenly. Set the cap on the head at a cheeky angle and sew in place with ladder stitch.

Snail

Green snails really do exist. Such a species is found in northern New Guinea where it lives amongst leaves in trees.

Materials: a 12″ (30.5 cm) square of green fur
small amount of stuffing
2 fabric circles each of 8″ (20 cm), 7″ (17.5 cm), 6″ (15 cm) and 5″ (12.5 cm) diameter
millinery elastic
2 trouser buttons
a 4″ (10 cm) circle of fabric
green felt for tentacles
2 pearl beads for eyes
2 circles of yellow felt 3″ (7.5 cm) in diameter
a 4″ (10 cm) circle of yellow felt
small length of braid for hat

Cutting: Make a pattern of the body from the pattern graph and cut two from fur fabric, remembering to reverse the pattern so as to cut a pair. Make a pattern of the tentacles, then cut two from green felt. Graph is on page 34.

Start by sewing the darts in both body pieces. Then place the latter together with right sides facing and sew around the edge, leaving A – B open for turning. Turn the body skin right side out and stuff firmly. Shape the base by pressing it flat against the table as you work. The snail should be able to stand. Close the opening.

The shell is made from the paired fabric circles. Gather these and flatten into discs as described for the millipede. Arrange them in a series, one on top of the other, forming a pyramid. Tie a short length of elastic to a trouser button and then thread the elastic through the centre of each disc. Tie the ends of the elastic around through the second trouser button. Place the shell on the back of the snail and ladder stitch the first, large fabric circle to the fur body so that the button is hidden and the shell is firmly anchored. The button at the apex of the shell is covered by the 4″ (10 cm) fabric circle. Prepare the latter by running a gathering thread around the edge and stuffing the circle. Place the remaining button amongst the stuffing and then close the circle.

Make a tentacle by rolling the felt into a stalk and slip stitching the edge. Sew a small pearl bead to one end as an eye. Sew the base of the tentacle to the side of the head. Work the second tentacle in the same way.

The hat is made from the yellow felt circles. Place the two smaller circles together and stitch, by hand or machine, around the edge. Gather the larger circle but only partially draw up. Fill the centre with stuffing, then sit this crown on the brim made from the smaller circles. Sew the crown and brim together, being careful to stitch through only one layer of the brim. Hide this row of stitches by laying a narrow braid over them. The hat is now ready to stitch to the head. Finally, groom the snail by releasing any fur that may be trapped in the seam.

More ideas for you to try

Rabbit — Join two fur balls like the panda and add rabbit-shaped ears.

Bear — Make as panda but in honey coloured fur, and omit the eye patches.

There are endless variations for using circles and you should have fun working out your own ideas. Advance to floppy toys with stuffed heads and disced bodies, arms, and legs.

5 The Scholars

Imagination is the keynote to this group of toys. They are simplicity itself and fun to make. Use them as an opportunity to experiment with shapes, fabrics and techniques, and create a range of characters. These scholars are named after early Greek and Renaissance philosophers and scientists, but they could equally well become a collection of clowns, famous explorers, or what have you. The pattern pieces given as suggestions for faces and limbs can all be interchanged, and the designs are based on a collection of ready made containers. By using a minimum of stitching and rather more glue, the shapes can be covered ready for the finishings to be added.

Materials: small pieces of fur, felt, leather, velvet, beads, wire, buttons, glue and cardboard. Glue the felt together and cut the patterns from a double layer. Leather is used single.

Shapes: tubes, yoghurt cartons, plastic containers, styrofoam balls and cones, tobacco tins, golf balls, sandwich spread pots or tins and cotton reels or spools, etc.

Aristotle

A cardboard roll, covered with fur, is the basic shape for Aristotle. His little pupils are cotton spools covered in the same way, with smaller, 'owlish' features. Aristotle was a scholar at Plato's Academy in Athens; he founded his own school, which became the first Lyceum, and gave lectures there every morning.

Cut a strip of fur, wide enough to cover the roll and to overlap at the top and bottom. Glue the strip to the roll and gather up the top and bottom, fastening off neatly so that the base is flat. Cut the face mask, beak, eyes, and wings from felt. (See graph page 40). Fringe the mask along lines marked. This makes the eyelashes. Put a spot of glue on the wrong side of the beak so that when the beak is pinched to-gether, just beneath the eyes, the glue will hold the pinch tight. Glue eyes in position at top of beak. Attach beak to face mask and glue all to the fur body. Fold wings in half and glue them together at the top. Attach to the body. Aristotle's pupils are made the same way, but cut small masks and beaks. There are no wings on these scholars. Sew loops to the top and then hang them from a branch.

Socrates

This Athenian teacher is formed around a sandwich spread pot. He is remembered for his concept of virtue and for the fact that Plato was one of his scholars.

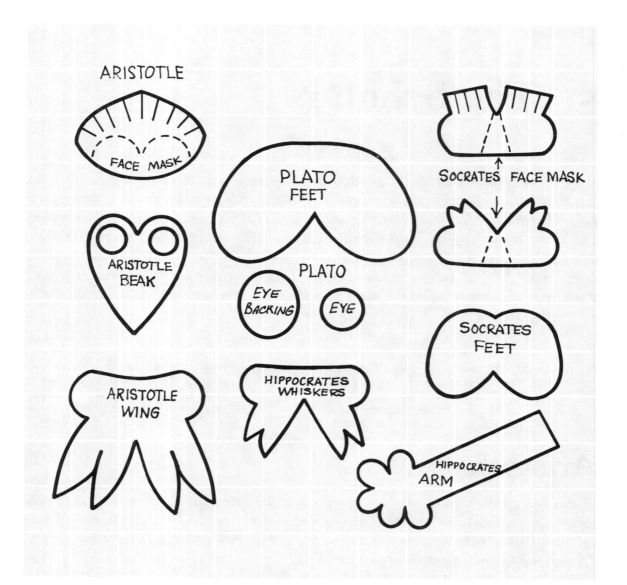

Pattern graph 2 The Scholars *one square = 1″ (2·5cm)*

Lay the container on a piece of fur and cut out a circle large enough to completely cover it. Gather the edge of the fur and draw up, fastening off on the underside. Cut out two feet and glue them, firstly together, then over the gathers on the underside of Socrates. Cut out eyes and face mask from felt. Fringe the mask to make eyebrows. Put a spot of glue in the centre of the mask and fold the two sides together, forming a nose bridge. Glue the eyes to either side of the nose, then glue the face to the body. An alternative face mask is given.

Copernicus

Copernicus is built around a florist's styrofoam ball. This Renaissance scientist furthered the theories of Pythagoras and made the sun the immovable centre of the universe with the earth and planets revolving around it.

40

Cut a circle of velvet large enough to cover a good half of the ball. Glue into place, being careful to spread any fullness as evenly as possible. Cut a felt face mask and sew a bead to the nose tab. Glue the mask to the ball so that the lower felt edge covers the raw edge of the velvet. Cut arms from felt and glue the top portion of each to either side of the face mask. Try to arrange them so that the hands lie across the tummy. Make the wig by sewing the fringe to the crown. Glue wig in position. Cut the eyes from felt and attach to the face.

Plato

A container similar to that used for Socrates, or a tobacco tin, is used to make Plato. A small amount of stuffing can be placed on top of the tin to cushion the hard edges. Plato founded the Academy in Athens, where he propounded his concept of democratic government.

Cover the frame in the same way as outlined for Socrates. The gathers are again hidden by a large pair of feet. Make a tail by covering a wire with felt. You can either glue the felt over the wire, or stitch a casing for it to lie in. Sew the tail to the base either under the feet or just behind them. A stitch may be needed to hold the tail against the side of the body. Cut the face mask from the pattern for Aristotle's wing. Turn it up the other way so that the long feathers become eyelashes. Glue eyes in place and sew a large bead or button on as a nose. Now glue the completed face to the body. Bend the tail into a twist.

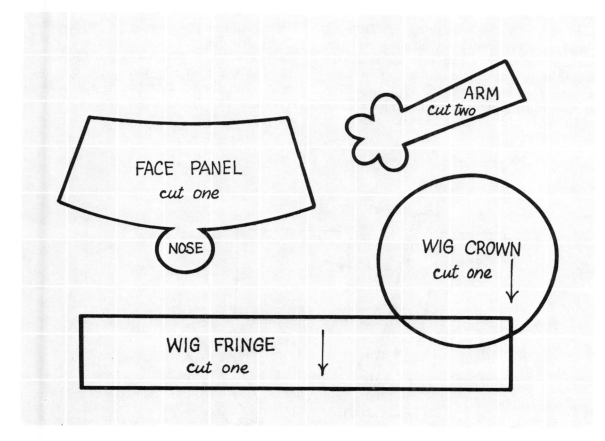

Pattern graph 3 Copernicus *one square = 1″ (2·5cm)*

41

Hippocrates

A styrofoam cone makes the base for Hippocrates. There were, in fact, seven Greek physicians of this name, but only one is immortalized in the Hippocratic Oath. He was the second.

Cut the tip off the cone with a serrated knife, as it makes an easier shape to work with. Lay a piece of felt against one side of the cone and glue in place. This becomes the front of the toy. Cut a piece of long fur to the shape outlined in Figure 17A, below, remembering to measure the cone to get the correct size.

Turn under and glue down the edges of both short sides, A B, and both long sides, C D. Now position fur around cone so that the two long sides overlap the edge of the felt apron, and glue in place. Fold the top down to cover the top edge of the felt apron. Stitch the folds in place. Cut a circle of felt to cover the base. To make the arms, first pierce the body from side to side through the fur and cone in the arm position with a steel knitting needle. Thread a length of wire through the channel made by the knitting needle. The wire for each arm should be long enough to double back on itself. Twist the wires together. Cut felt arms similar to Copernicus, but make them just a little wider, with five fingers at the end. (See page 40). Lay glue along the arm, then fold over the wire and hold in place until firmly stuck. Bend arms into any position required.

The face has two sets of whiskers. The longer whiskers use the wing pattern for Aristotle while the shorter whiskers use the face mask pattern for Socrates. These are used upside down for this toy. Glue them together at the top only. Cut a nose of double felt measuring $2\frac{1}{2}''$ (6.5 cm) by $1\frac{1}{2}''$ (4 cm) for a face mask of the above size. Roll each short side towards the centre, then catch them together with a slip stitch on the underside. The two enclosed rolls represent nostrils and generally give the nose a firmer shape (see Figure 17B, below). Anchor the nose to the centre top of the combined whiskers by sewing on either side. Check that the nose projects outwards and is securely attached. Now cover the stitches on the side of the nose by gluing the eyes over them. Glue the finished face to the body to cover the join between fur and top of felt apron.

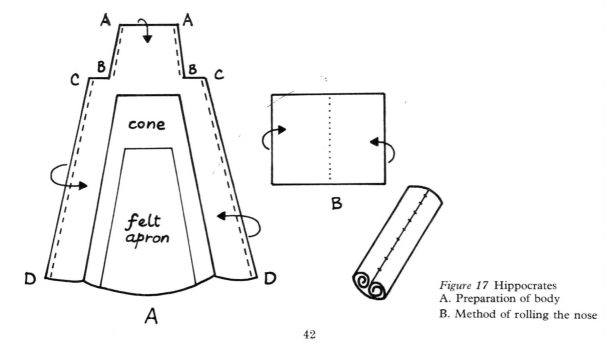

Figure 17 Hippocrates
A. Preparation of body
B. Method of rolling the nose

Another idea for you to try

Cover a cylinder with fur fabric and then add all the faces of the scholars to it, making a totem pole. I would call this character Pythagoras, for he was a philosopher, politician, mathematician, and scientist: a little bit of everything, which also describes the totem.

Choose a tall cylinder, like a detergent container, and either fill it with stones to weigh it down for a standing toy or leave it empty and hang as a mobile.

The crowning figure of a totem is usually Thunderbird. The flapping of his wings is supposed to darken the sky while the rolling of his eyes causes thunder and lightning. You could start with Aristotle at the top, followed by all the others, and some of your own designs.

6 Bean Bags

The mobility and floppiness of bean bags allows the toys to assume a wide range of movements and attitudes, some of which can be very realistic. It is the stuffing material which gives the toy its flexibility, and in this instance dried rice has been used. Because the rice is so heavy, seams need to be extra strong and the toy should be small enough to hold comfortably in the hand.

Crab

The largest of all crabs is a spider crab with legs that span over twelve feet. The crab given here measures 6″ (15 cm) from claw tip to claw tip.

Materials:
a 7″ (17·5 cm) square of patterned fabric
a 7″ (17·5 cm) square of plain fabric
a 6″ (15 cm) square of felt
4 ozs (112 g) dried rice
2 beads for eyes

Cutting:
Make the pattern by enlarging the body and legs from the pattern graph. Cut the back of the body from patterned fabric and the front of the body from plain fabric. The leg strips are cut from felt.

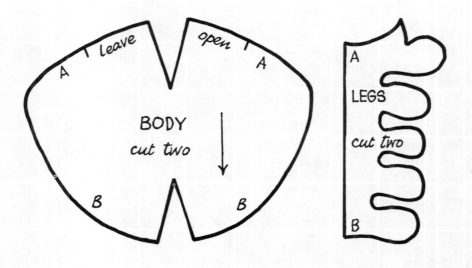

Pattern graph 4   Crab *one square = 1″ (2·5cm)*

44

Commence by sewing the darts on both body pieces. Place a felt leg strip on the body back, matching A to A and B to B. It should be laid on the right side of the material with the legs pointing inwards. Sew in place and repeat for the second leg strip. Place front and back bodies together, with right sides facing, and sew from A through B then from B to A. Turn right side out. Fill the crab with rice. You will find it easier to do this if you use a funnel. Close the opening. Sew the two beads to the top of the head so that the crab appears alert.

Snake

The longest snake is undoubtedly the South American anaconda. A length of $37\frac{1}{2}$ feet was recorded from a captured specimen. The snake given here measures a mere two feet.

Materials: 4″ (10 cm) of 48″ (122 cm) wide fabric
small piece of red felt for tongue
1 lb (454 g) dried rice
2 large beads for eyes

Fold the fabric strip in half with the right sides and both the selvedges together. Now machine the outline of a snake on this strip by making a broad head end and a tapering tail end. Remember to leave an opening for turning. Trim away all excess material and turn the skin right side through. The seams mark the centre top and centre bottom of the snake. Form a mouth by pushing in the broad end of the snake with your finger. Lay the felt tongue on the floor of the mouth and machine through both thicknesses of fabric (see Figure 18, below). Insert the funnel in the opening and fill the snake with rice. Leave just enough slack so that the snake may be coiled. Close the opening. It only remains to stitch the beads on the head. Use the centre top seam as a guide and place the eyes 2″ (5 cm) back from the mouth.

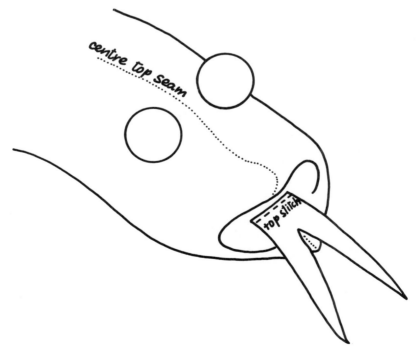

Figure 18 Construction of snake's head

Frog

The Goliath frog of West Africa holds the record for being the largest. When the legs are fully stretched out, it measures 24″ (61 cm). The frog given here measures 8″ (20 cm) when extended.

Materials: a 10″ (25.5 cm) square of patterned fabric
a 10″ (25.5 cm) square of taffeta
8 ozs (227 g) dried rice
2 pearl beads for eyes

Cutting: Make the pattern by enlarging that given in the pattern graph. Do not cut the fabric.

Place the two squares of fabric together with right sides facing. Pin each of the corners. Now lay the pattern on the plain fabric and draw around it with a soft pencil. This line acts as a sewing guide. Machine around the frog, twice, paying particular attention to the corners. Leave an opening between the legs for turning. Remove the pins from the corners of the fabric and trim excess material away from the frog outline. Clip carefully into corners of the legs and arms. Turn the skin through the opening by gently pushing the limbs with the blunt end of a pencil. Place a funnel in the opening and fill the tummy with rice. Remove the funnel and temporarily close the opening with a pin. Work the rice into each arm. Hold it in place by making a row of tiny running stitches across the shoulder line on each side.

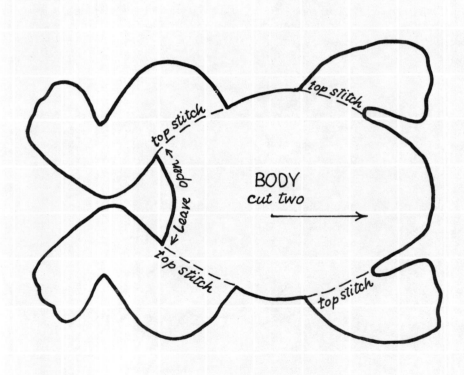

Pattern graph 5 Frog *one square = 1″ (2·5cm)*

46

Work rice into the legs in the same way and again hold the rice in place by working a row of stitches across the tops of the legs. Guide lines are marked on the pattern for your convenience. Remove the pin from the opening and fill the frog with more rice. Leave just enough space to make the frog pliable. Close the opening securely. Attach the eyes to either side of the head.

Ladybird

The ladybird described here is the familiar form – seven black spots on red wings. You might well like to make a series of different ladybirds. Try the following forms – red wings with either two black spots or ten black spots, black wings with either two red spots or ten red spots and lastly, yellow wings with twenty-two black spots.

Materials:
a 9″ (23 cm) square of black felt
a 9″ (23 cm) square of red felt
8 ozs (227 g) dried rice
2 flat pearl buttons for eyes

Cutting:
Make a pattern from the pattern graph. Cut base, head, seven spots, and two small pupils from black felt. Cut two wings from red felt.

Commence by sewing the dart on the head. Sew both wings together from A to B. Place head to wings with right sides together, matching A to A and C to C, and sew. Insert base, matching D to D and B to B, and sew. Leave a small opening on one side as indicated on the pattern. Turn skin right side out and fill with rice. Close the opening. Cover the wings with the black spots, only do remember to place them symmetrically. These may be either glued or stitched in place. Anchor the buttons to the face and stick on small black felt pupils.

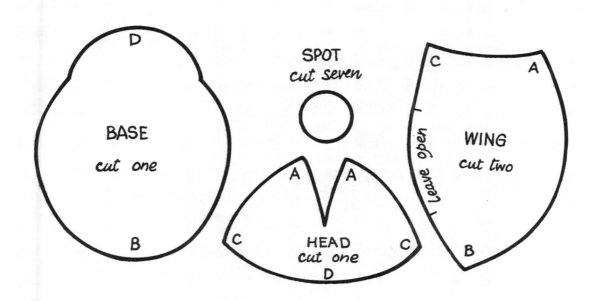

Pattern graph 6 Ladybird *one square = 1″ (2·5cm)*

7 Nursery Toys

As children develop their skills and become more aware of their surroundings, so will their interest in toys increase. In the very early days, texture is of paramount importance. A favourite toy is one that is touched by mouth, chewed, and sucked just as much as it is touched by hand. Soft furry toys are very comforting and warm compared to cold plastic ones. Colours, eyes, size, noise, and identification of the toy as a domestic animal or nursery rhyme character all become significant at some time during the child's development. Indeed, soft toys are the child's companion and comforter during the night and at moments of distress.
The nursery toys designed here are all of comparable size, and for this reason you will be able to interchange the heads and create many more characters than the seven described here in detail.

Elephant, Dog, and Donkey

These three animals have been closely associated with man as working animals for a very long time. An ancient King of Persia is reputed to have had an army of 9,000 elephants, and you will have heard how Hannibal set off across the Alps with 50 elephants to capture Italy. The donkey is probably derived from the wild Nubian asses of North East Africa while the ass of the Bible is in all probability the onager of the Middle East. Dogs are the most domesticated of the three animals. As well as being used for work, they are small enough to be taken into the home and kept as pets, purely for pleasure.

Elephant

Materials: an 18″ (46 cm) square of fur fabric
pair of 14 mm safety eyes
6 ozs (170 g) stuffing

Cutting: Make the pattern by enlarging that shown in the pattern graph. Place the body pattern on folded paper as directed. You will then have a complete pattern to work from, which is much easier when cutting fur. Cut the head as a pair, one side being reversed. Cut two pairs of ears. The finished elephant stands 8″ (20 cm) high.

3 Bean Bags (opposite)
From top: frog, snake, crab, frog, ladybird.

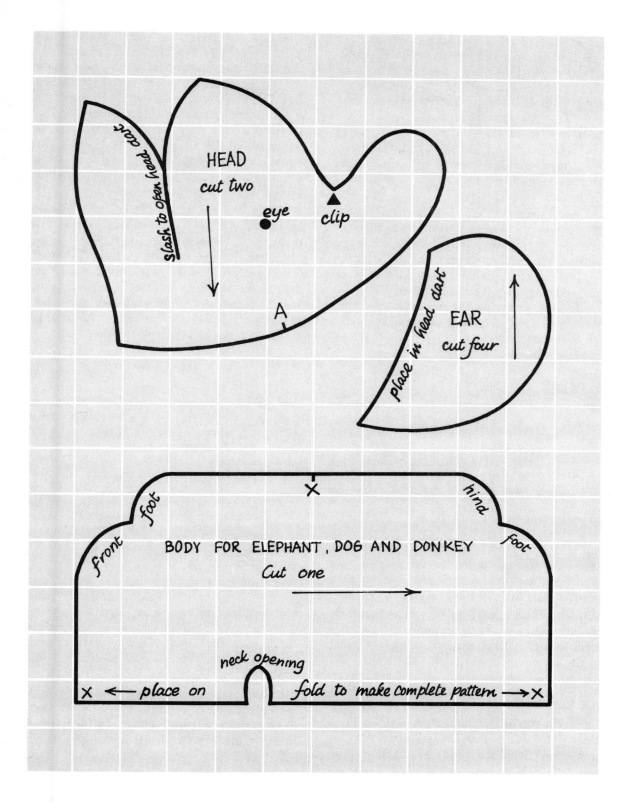

HEAD
cut two

eye

clip

slash to open head dart

A

EAR
cut four

place in head dart

BODY FOR ELEPHANT, DOG AND DONKEY

Cut one

front foot

hind foot

X

neck opening

X ← place on   fold to make complete pattern → X

Pattern graph 7 Elephant *one square = 1″ (2·5cm)*

4 Nursery Toys (opposite)
Top: kitten. *Middle, from left to right:* rabbit, fox, teddy. *Bottom:* donkey, dog, rabbit, elephant.

Prepare the ears first by placing right sides of each pair together and sewing round the outer curved edge. Turn them right side out and baste each ear in position in a head dart. Bring both sides of head darts together and sew. Tug the ears to check that they are securely stitched in. Now place both sides of head together with right sides facing and sew from the neck edge beneath the trunk at A, working around the head to the neck edge at the back.

Clip the curve and angle of the trunk as indicated on the pattern. Turn the head right side out. If you are using safety lock in eyes, then now is the time to insert them. Stuff the head by working small amounts into the trunk first and then into the head proper. Close the opening by gathering up the neck edge and fastening off securely. Put the head aside for the moment.

The body is stitched in four identical stages. Take one corner, which is the foot of the body, and fold it over so that the Xs on either side of the foot come together with right sides facing. Sew from the corner to the Xs. Repeat this stage on the remaining three corners, so that all the Xs come together in the centre on the underside of the body. Turn body right side out through the neck opening and stuff. Close neck opening by gathering the edge and pulling up the thread. Fasten off.

With this pattern, the head can be positioned in a variety of ways. As well as looking forwards or to either side, the head may also be placed so that the elephant looks up or down. Select the position you want, then place head over the neck gathers and ladder stitch it to the body. Felt eyes or embroidered eyes are worked at this stage. Finish by releasing any fur trapped in the seams and brushing thoroughly.

Dog

Materials: 12″ (30.5 cm) × 9″ (23 cm) black fur
18″ (46 cm) × 12″ (30.5 cm) white fur
pair of 16 mm safety eyes
6 ozs (170 g) stuffing

Cutting: Make the pattern by enlarging that shown in the pattern graph. Use the body pattern given for the elephant. The finished dog stands 8″ (20 cm) high. Cut the ears, tail, and face panels from the black fur. The remaining parts of the dog are cut from white fur.

Fold each ear in half lengthways and sew across the top and down the side, leaving the base open for turning through. Baste ears in position, one to the top edge of each face panel.

Sew the head gusset to one face panel by placing right sides together and stitching from front to back. Attach the remaining face panel in the same way to the other side of the head gusset. Now position the snout and head together by matching A to A and sewing. Fold the snout in half and sew from B to A. Stitch across the top of the snout from C to C. Turn head right side out and insert safety eyes at this stage. Stuff the head, paying particular attention to the snout. Gather up the neck opening and fasten off.

Make the body by following the instructions given for the elephant. Fold the tail in half and sew the edge, leaving the base open for turning through. Stuff tail lightly and then ladder stitch it to the body. Place head in desired position and ladder stitch it to the body as well.

Finish the dog by working a nose and mouth with black stranded cotton. The nose is a block of satin stitch. Finally, release any fur trapped in the seams and brush the coat.

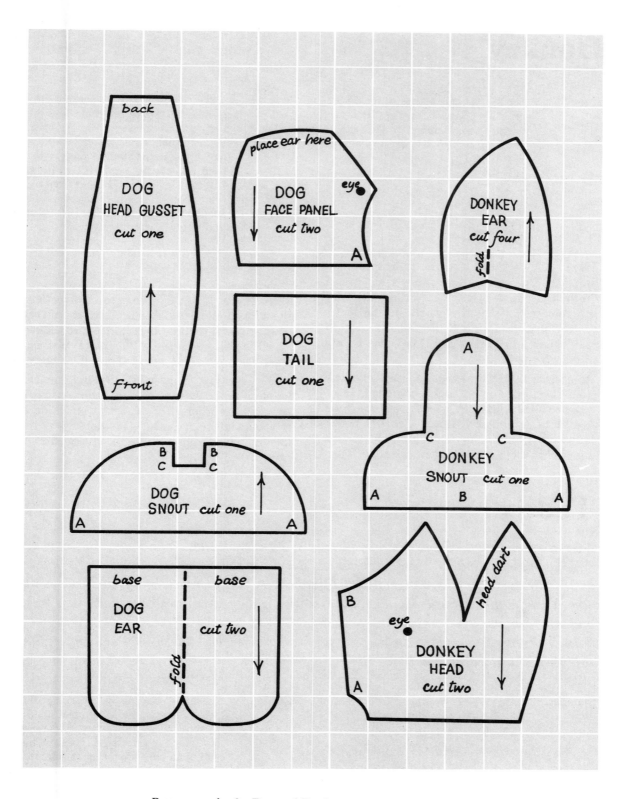

Pattern graph   8   Dog and Donkey *one square = 1″ (2·5cm)*

51

Donkey

Materials: an 18″ (46 cm) square of fur fabric
a 9″ (23 cm) square of fur for
snout and ear lining
pair of 14 mm safety eyes
6 ozs (170 g) stuffing
18″ (46 cm) braid

Cutting: Make the pattern by enlarging that shown in the pattern graph. Use the body pattern given for the elephant. The finished donkey stands 8″ (20 cm) high. Remember to reverse the head and ear patterns when cutting. Cut the ear lining and snout from the same colour fur. The tail consists of a small rectangle of main colour fur and a tuft of contrasting fur.

Make each ear by placing the right sides of a lining to an outer ear piece and sewing around the outer edge. Turn the ears right side out and fold in half lengthways. Baste the lower edge so that the fold is held in place. Position each ear in a head dart and then sew securely in place.

Now place both side heads together and sew from the front to the back neck edge. Place snout to head with right sides facing, matching A to B to A, and sew. Make the darts in the snout by sewing C to A on both sides. Sew under chin seam down to the neck edge. Turn head right side out and finish as for the elephant.

Make the body by following the instructions given for the elephant. Arrange the head on the body and sew the two together. Make the tail by rolling the rectangle of fur into a tube and sewing on the tuft at the tip. Sew tail to body.

The harness is constructed by looping the braid around the snout and then passing a second loop around the head and attaching it to the snout loop. Finish your donkey by releasing any trapped fur and giving him a brushing.

Teddy

No collection of toys for small children would be complete without a bear, for these animals have completely captured their imagination. Bears are related to dogs and racoons, but in contrast frequently prefer a vegetable diet like berries, grasses, roots, honey, and fruit, with occasional additions of fish and meat. An exception is the polar bear who feeds on seals, fish, and other sea food.

There are several very different patterns for bears in the book, this one being a simple, flat teddy with hinged arms and legs.

Materials: an 18″ (46 cm) square of fur fabric
8 ozs (227 g) stuffing
pair of 14 mm safety eyes

Cutting: Make a pattern by enlarging the pattern graph. For a complete body pattern, place the enlarged pattern on folded paper as directed. This will open out, when cut, to full size. The finished teddy is 13″ (33 cm) tall.

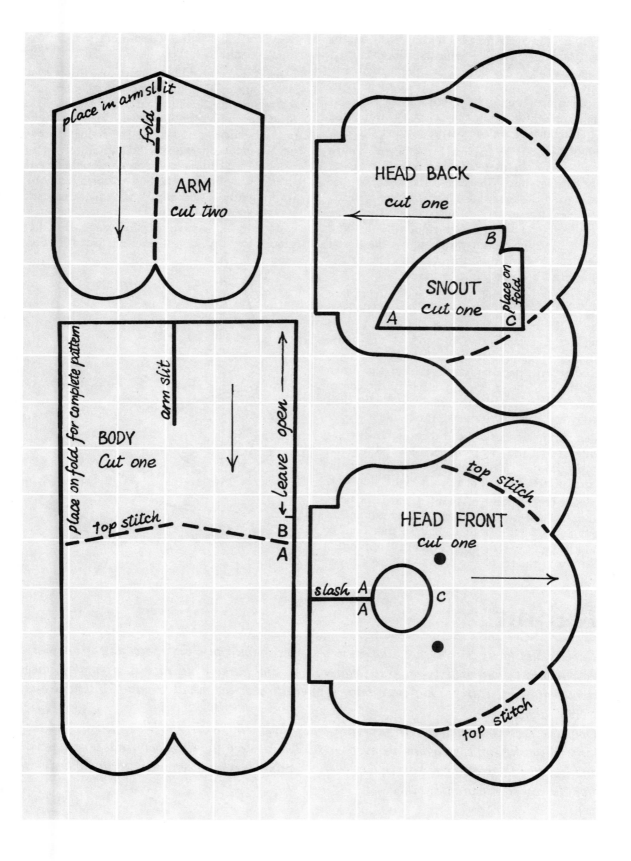

place in arm slit

fold

ARM
cut two

HEAD BACK

cut one

B

SNOUT
cut one

place on fold

A   C

place on fold for complete pattern

arm slit

BODY
Cut one

leave open

top stitch

B
A

top stitch

HEAD FRONT
cut one

slash A

A   C

top stitch

Prepare the arms first by folding each one in half lengthways and sewing the outer curved edge on the wrong side. Turn them right side out through the open base. Fill them with stuffing to within one inch of the opening and hold the stuffing in place away from the opening by sewing a few large tacking stitches.

Fold the body in half by bringing the centre back edges together, and sew from A to B on the wrong side. Now refold the body so that you bring the inner leg edges together for each leg. Sew leg seams from the bottom foot edge to the top. Turn the legs right side out and stuff. Machine or stab stitch across the top of the legs as marked on the pattern. The stitching forms a hinge joint for the legs.

Place an arm in each arm slit and sew in place on the wrong side. Check that arms are secure by pulling them. Now close the shoulders by making a seam across the top of the body, sloping it gently on either side of the neck. Remove the tacking stitches from the arms. Stuff the body and close the rest of the centre back seam with ladder stitch. Put the finished body aside while you make the head.

Place front and back head together with right sides facing and sew from neck edge, round the entire head, to neck edge. Clip corners at the base of the ears. Turn head right side out.

Match centre point of snout, C, to C of head and sew the two together. Turn head inside out and fold the front in half so that the Ds and Es come together (see Figure 19, opposite). Sew from the tip of the nose to the neck edge.

Sew across the point of the snout to close the small opening.

Turn head right side out again and insert eyes at this stage. Top stitch the base of each ear, following the guide line marked on the pattern. Stuff the head firmly, pushing out the cheeks on each side and moulding the snout. Gather up the neck opening to hold the stuffing in place. Use a completely separate double thread to stitch the head to the body. Finish teddy by working a nose and mouth with black or dark brown stranded cotton. Embroidered or felt eyes can be worked at this stage. Finally, groom the toy and if wanted, tie a ribbon around his neck.

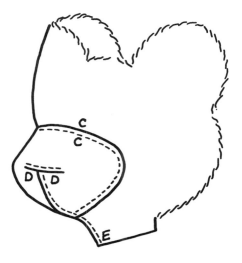

Figure 19 Position of seams in snout

Rabbit

Rabbits and hares are rodents, like squirrels, mice, guinea pigs and porcupines. They are vegetarians feeding mainly on grass, clover, corn and bark. Wild rabbits originally came from south-west Europe, but since have spread all over the world, even to Australia and New Zealand.

Domestic rabbits include the Angora with lovely long white hair, the Blue Vienna, and the large Flemish Giant, weighing many pounds. The pattern for this rabbit has hinged arms and legs like those of the teddy. In addition, a seating dart has been included in the body to give the toy even more flexibility.

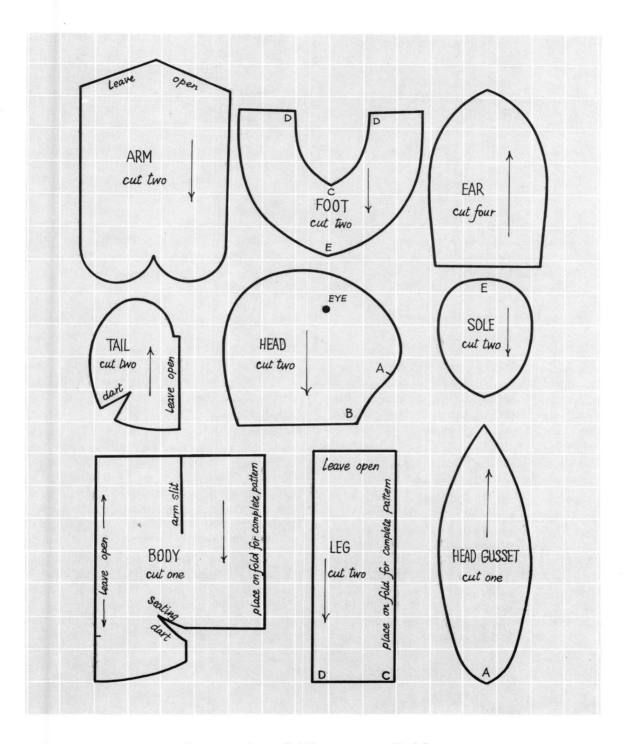

Pattern graph 10   Rabbit *one square = 1″ (2·5cm)*

Materials: a 24″ (61 cm) square of fur for body
pair of 16 mm safety eyes
10 ozs (280 g) stuffing
a 12″ (30·5 cm) square of contrasting fur

Cutting: Make a pattern from the pattern graph, page 55. Place body and leg pattern on folded paper as directed, to make a complete pattern. Cut the head as a pair, reversing the pattern. The main part of the rabbit is cut from one colour fur while the tail, ear linings, and soles of the feet are cut from contrasting coloured fur.
The finished rabbit measures 20″ (51 cm) from the tips of his ears to his feet.

Place the two head pieces together with right sides facing and sew the short seam from A to B. Insert head gusset and baste in position before sewing. Close the remaining seam at the centre back of the head. Turn head right side out and insert eyes. Stuff head firmly and close neck opening by gathering it up.

Assemble the ears by sewing a lining to an outer ear piece on the wrong side. Turn right side out and fold in raw edge, slip stitching the opening. Fold the ears at their base to make a tuck, then ladder stitch them to either side of the head using the seams as a guide for positioning them. Put head aside and work on the body.

Sew the two small seating darts first, then close the centre back seam for an inch at the base.

Prepare the legs by matching C and Ds of each foot to leg, and sew. Sew the centre back seam of the foot and leg. Insert soles, matching Es, and sew. Turn legs right side out and stuff to within one inch of the top leg opening. Hold the stuffing in place with giant tacking stitches as you did for the teddy's arm. Now insert each leg through the bottom of the body so that the feet emerge by the neck. Baste in position, then turn body through to check that

this is correctly done. Turn wrong side out again and machine across the line of basting several times to make really secure.

Fold each arm in half and sew the outer edge. Turn through the top and stuff the arms to within one inch of the opening. Hold the stuffing in place with large tacking stitches. Place an arm in each arm slit of the body and sew. Check that the arms are secure by pulling them. Sew across the top of the body to form shoulders on either side of the neck. Stuff body firmly and close the centre back seam with ladder stitch.

Make the tail by first sewing the small darts in each half, then joining together on the wrong side. Leave the straight edge open for turning through. Clip the angle and turn; stuff firmly. Close the opening by gathering up, then position tail on the body and ladder stitch in place. If you take care in placing the tail, your rabbit will be able to sit up by himself.

Remove the tacking stitches from the tops of the arms and legs. Now work a nose and mouth on the face with stranded cotton and add the alternative eyes if necessary. Finally, groom the rabbit by brushing and releasing any fur trapped in the seams.

Fox and Kitten

Both these animals belong to the large group of meat-eating mammals, the carnivores. The cat family includes the more familiar lion, tiger, and leopard, as well as the lesser known ocelot, lynx, serval, and caffer cat. Foxes belong to the dog family, together with true dogs, hunting dogs, and the maned wolf.
These two toys share the same simple body pattern but have separate head and tail patterns.

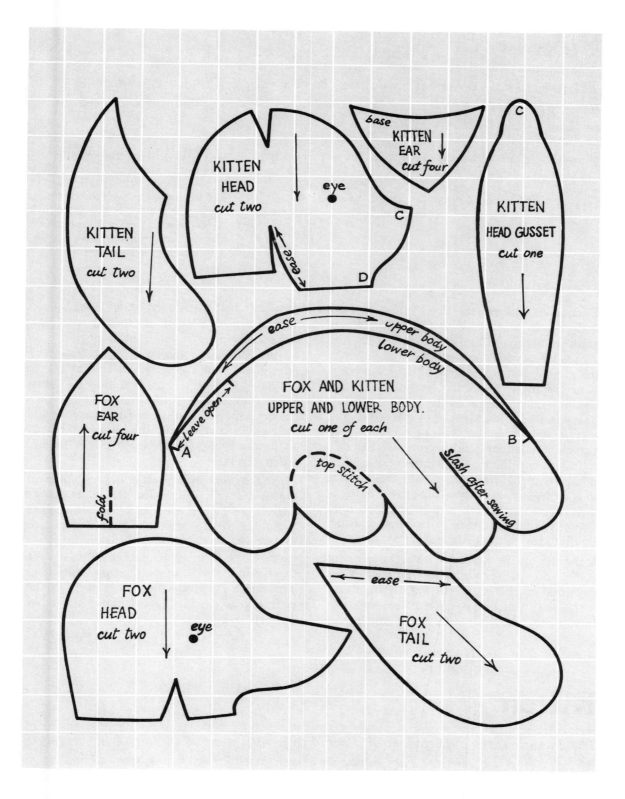

Pattern graph 11   Fox and Kitten *one square = 1" (2·5cm)*

57

Fox

The common fox has thick fur which may be very variable in colour, although we tend to think of it as reddish coloured. The Arctic fox, on the other hand, has a summer greyish coloured coat and a winter white coat.

Materials:
an 18″ (46 cm) square of reddish fur fabric
8 ozs (227 g) stuffing
pair of 16 mm safety eyes
a 6″ (15 cm) square of white fur

Cutting:
Make the pattern by enlarging that shown on page 57. Follow the outer line for the upper body and the inner line for the lower body. The finished fox measures 10″ (25·5 cm) from tip of snout to tip of tail. Cut all the pieces from the main colour fur and the ear linings from white fur.

Commence making the fox by placing both body pieces together with right sides facing and sewing around the legs from A to B. Run an easing thread along the back edge of the upper body and pull it up to fit the lower body. Now sew the two together on the wrong side, leaving an opening near the tail for turning. You will find it much easier to stitch the front legs if you leave the slashing till last. Clip curves and corners and turn the body skin right side out. Place a small amount of stuffing in the inner back leg. Now hold this stuffing in place by stitching across the top of the leg as marked on the pattern. Do this on the right side of the fabric, either by machine or hand. Stuff the rest of the body, but do not close.

Make the tail by placing both right sides together and sewing round the outer edge. Turn right side out. Pleat the base slightly and insert in the body. Catch in position at the same time as you close the body with ladder stitch.

Sew the small cheek darts on both head pieces and then place both sides together with right sides facing and sew from the front neck edge all the way round the head to the back neck edge. Turn head right side out and insert eyes at this stage. Stuff the head carefully by inserting small amounts in the snout first and then the head proper. Gather up the neck edge and fasten off securely. Place the head on the body so that the snout rests on the front legs. Ladder stitch in place.

Make the ears by placing a lining and outer ear together and sewing round the outer curved edge. Turn right side out and fold raw edges in and close. Attach ears to the head so that your fox appears alert. Felt or embroidered eyes are added at this stage. Work a small group of satin stitches in black cotton on the tip of the snout. This makes a very effective nose. Finally, groom your toy as already described for the other nursery toys.

Kitten

The domestic cat is a descendant of the wild caffer cat, races of which still live in North Africa, Syria, and Arabia. They have been domesticated for at least 4,000 years although they were not common as household pets in Europe until the 1700s. Playful kittens fascinate little children with their antics, so it is no wonder that they figure frequently in nursery rhymes and make very acceptable toys.

Materials: an 18″ (46 cm) square of fur fabric
8 ozs (227 g) stuffing
pair of 16 mm safety eyes
small piece of pink satin for ears

Cutting: Make the pattern by enlarging that on page 57. The finished kitten measures 10″ (25·5 cm) from front legs to tip of tail. Cut all pieces from fur, remembering to cut a pair of ear, tail, and head pieces by reversing the pattern. Cut ear linings from satin.

Commence making the kitten by sewing and stuffing the body, following the instructions given for the fox. Place right sides of tail pieces together and sew around the outside curve. Turn tail right side through and stuff.

Insert in the body opening and secure at the same time as you close the body with ladder stitch.

The pouched cheeks of the kitten are made by easing the long side of the cheek dart to fit the short side. Do this with the darts on both sides of the head and make the more straightforward darts on the top of the head as well. Place right sides of both head pieces together and stitch from C to D. Insert the head gusset and baste in place on both sides first. Check that it is even before sewing. Turn head right side out and insert eyes at this stage. Stuff the head, paying particular attention to the cheek pouches. Close the neck opening and ladder stitch head to body.

Place ear lining to ear and sew outer curved edge. Turn right side out, fold in raw edges and sew ear to head so that it is curved, framing the face. Make second ear in the same way. Work a nose and mouth with three strands of pink embroidery cotton.

By using short or long fur, you can make short-haired or Persian kittens, and using different colours you can make further variations.

Further ideas for you to try

The seven nursery toys have only four different body patterns between them. By interchanging the heads and tails you can considerably increase the number of toys possible from these few patterns. When putting different heads on the rabbit body, slightly increase their size to keep the toy in proportion. Do this by cutting $\frac{1}{8}$″ (3 mm) outside the pattern. The following table shows 24 possible arrangements.

Head Pattern	Body Pattern			
	Elephant	Teddy	Rabbit	Fox
Elephant	√	√	—	√
Dog	√	√	√	√
Donkey	√	√	—	√
Teddy	—	√	√	—
Rabbit	√	√	√	√
Fox	√	√	√	√
Kitten	√	√	√	√

8　Mice and Moles

The animals in this section are small, furry, timid creatures. None of them is easily seen, yet there are often signs to show us where they have been. Moles leave mounds of earth above their underground highways, while nibbled cheese can tell us where the mice were last night.

Mole

Moles, together with hedgehogs and shrews, are small, short-legged mammals known as Insectivores because they feed for the most part on insects, larvae, and worms. Moles are nocturnal animals, doing most of their digging at night with the powerful claws on their front legs.

Materials:
$\frac{1}{4}$ yd (23 cm) of 36″ (91 cm) wide needlecord (twill)
a 9″ (23 cm) square of felt
10 ozs (280 g) stuffing
black and white felt for eyes

Cutting:
Make the pattern by enlarging that shown in the pattern graph. The finished mole is 12″ (30·5 cm) long. Cut the body from needlecord, reversing the body to make a pair. Cut the feet from felt.

Place the two body pieces together with right sides facing and sew from A forward to the nose and along the back to B. Now take each pair of felt feet and in turn, stitch along the guide line as marked on the pattern. Trim away excess felt on the front feet to form the claws. Lightly stuff each foot then baste feet in position on the base piece of fabric. They should lie on the right side of the fabric and be directed inwards. Place base to body, matching A to A and B to B, and sew, leaving an opening for turning. Trim and clip the top back seam. Turn skin right side out. Stuff firmly, starting with the nose and working back to the body. Close opening with ladder stitch. Glue the eyes together, then glue them to the head.

For a change, make the mole in velvet, and if the toy is for an older child, add some fine whiskers to either side of the nose.

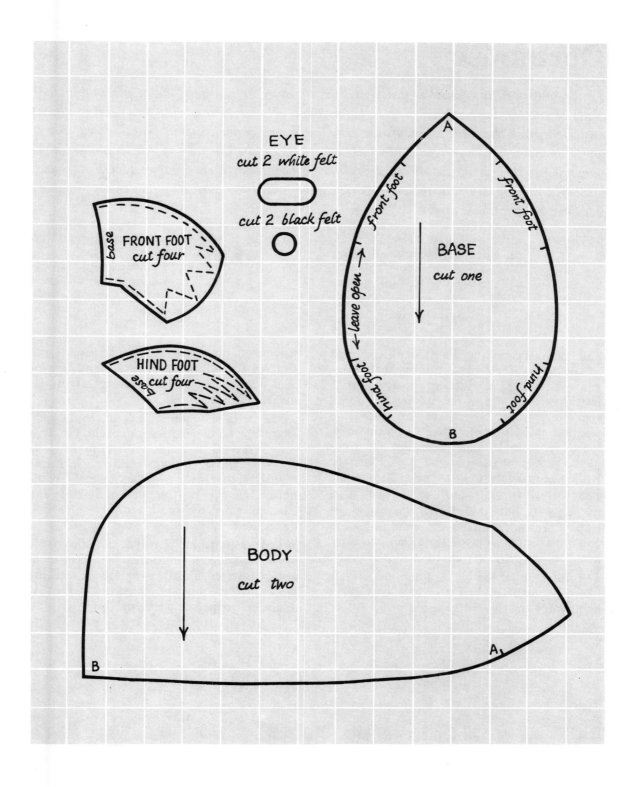

EYE
cut 2 white felt
cut 2 black felt

FRONT FOOT
cut four

base

HIND FOOT
cut four

base

BASE
cut one

A

front foot

front foot

← leave open →

hind foot

hind foot

B

BODY
cut two

B

A

Pattern graph 12   Mole *one square = 1″ (2·5cm)*

61

Dormouse

This exquisite little animal is a rodent, like the harvest mouse. Rodents account for one third of all the land mammals. They are found all over the world, able to live almost anywhere from the coldest to warmest regions, on the ground and in trees, in and out of water. Dormice can be recognized by their long, bushy tails. They are excellent climbers, even managing to do this upside down. They live in hedgerows and in burrows in the ground, but build their nests in the undergrowth. Winter finds them curled up fast asleep, for dormice are hibernating animals.

Materials: an 18″ (46 cm) square of fur fabric
pair of 20 mm brown safety eyes
8 ozs (227 g) stuffing
6″ (15 cm) × 12″ (30.5 cm) woollen fabric

Cutting: Make the pattern by enlarging that shown in the pattern graph. This makes a dormouse sitting 8″ (20 cm) high. Cut main body from fur fabric, reversing one side to make a pair. The ear linings are cut from the woollen fabric.

Commence by making the darts on each half of the body. Then place the two halves together with right sides facing and sew from A to B. Leave an opening for turning, just above the tail position. Safety eyes are locked in position at this time. Place base to body, matching A to B, and sew. Turn the completed skin right side out and stuff. Put aside while you make the tail and ears.

Fold the tail in half lengthways and sew from the tapered end towards the short straight edge. Turn right side out. Place tail in bottom half of the stuffing opening and close the latter at the same time as sewing the tail in securely.

The tail is rather too fat for a dormouse if left like this but by folding it in half lengthways and closing the two sides together with ladder stitch you can make the tail act as its own stuffing. By pulling up ever so slightly on the ladder stitch you will also incorporate a permanent curl in the tail.

Make each ear by placing a lining to the right side of the fur ear and sewing around the outer edge. Turn ear right side out, fold in the lower raw edge and close with ladder stitch, gently pulling on the thread to gather the ear. Lay the finished ear over the front dart of the body and stitch in place by working ladder stitch first down the front of the ear, then the back.

Wired eyes or padded felt eyes are added to the toy at this stage if so desired. Whiskers could also be inserted. Finally groom the toy, giving it a gentle brushing and releasing any fur that might be trapped in the seams.

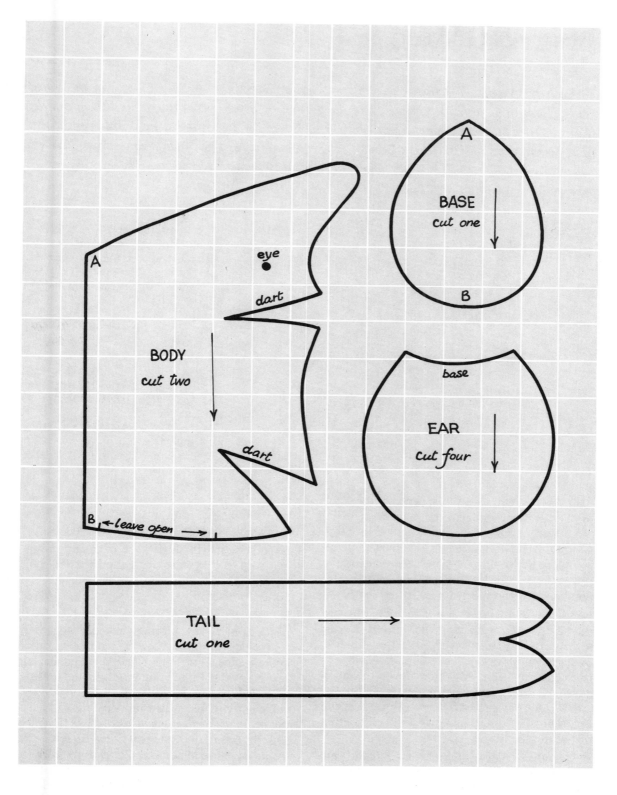

Pattern graph 13   Dormouse *one square = 1″ (2·5cm)*

63

Harvest Mice

These little rodents live in open country, often amongst high grasses or in oat and wheat fields. They are excellent climbers, like the dormouse, using their tails to hold them to grass stalks as they clamber about. Their summer nests are built up grass stems, while winter time finds them living in runs in the ground or in outbuildings. The harvest mice given here are mother and daughter. They are made in hessian, which would seem to be in keeping for animals which feed on grain.

Materials: 3½″ (9 cm) × 18″ (46 cm) felt for mother's tail
3″ (7·5 cm) × 12″ (30·5 cm) felt for daughter's tail
½ yd (46 cm) of 50″ (127 cm) wide hessian (burlap)
1½ lbs (681 g) stuffing
felt for eye backing and nose
black and white felt for eyes
½ yd (46 cm) of 36″ (91 cm) wide gingham
¼ yd (23 cm) velvet
¼ yd (23 cm) taffeta

Cutting: Make patterns from the pattern graph. Mother stands 13″ (33 cm) tall and daughter stands 9″ (23 cm) tall. Cut one body, four ears and one base from hessian for each harvest mouse.
Mother's apron:
strap 48″ (122 cm) × 3½″ (9 cm), skirt 10″ (25·5 cm) × 5″ (12·5 cm).
Daughter's apron:
strap 36″ (91 cm) × 2½″ (6·5 cm), skirt 7″ (17.5 cm) × 4″ (10 cm).
Cut the aprons from gingham or other cotton.
Cut the cape from velvet and lining from taffeta.
Cut daughter's eyes slightly smaller than the pattern.

The body skins, features, and aprons for mother and daughter are both worked in the same way, so the instructions are for either toy. Mother harvest mouse has a velvet cape to complete her outfit. Hessian has a tendency to fray, so you must neaten all raw edges and double stitch the seams for added strength.

Make the tail first so that it is ready to put into the centre back seam. Cut the tail felt in half, lengthways, lay the two strips together and fold in half, lengthways. You will now have four thicknesses of felt. Machine down the open edge of the strip and shape a tapered end to the tail. Trim away excess felt from the end of the tail. The tail now has its own built-in stuffing of the doubled layers of felt.

Fold body in half, right sides facing, and sew from A to B. Leave an opening for turning and remember to insert the tail near the end of the seam. Insert base, matching B to B, and baste. Turn skin right side out to check that the base is evenly inserted. If you are satisfied, then turn wrong side out and sew in place. Turn skin right side out again and stuff very firmly.

Keep standing the body on a table and dumping it up and down to make the base flat. This is very necessary if you want your harvest mouse to stand when it is finished. Close opening with ladder stitch.

Make the ears by placing each pair together, right sides facing, and sewing around the outer curved edge. Turn right side out and neaten raw base edge by turning in fabric and closing with ladder stitch. Pull on the thread just sufficiently to make the ears curve into a pleasing petaloid shape. This helps to make the mice slightly feminine whereas ungathered ears would be more masculine. Position the ears on either side of the centre back seam, so that they frame the face. Sew in place very securely as the mice are sure to be lifted and carried about by their ears.

5 Mice and Moles (opposite)
From top, moving clockwise: dormouse, mother harvest mouse, mole, daughter harvest mouse.

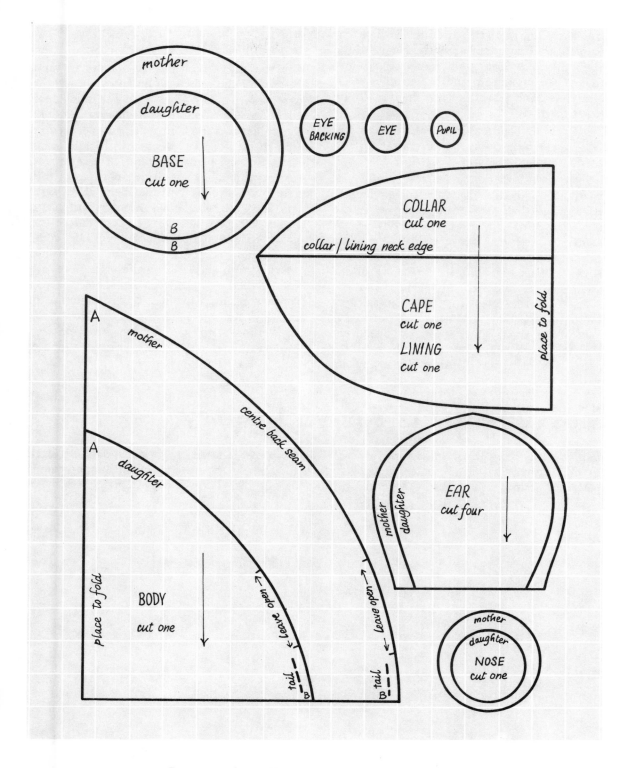

Pattern graph 14   Harvest Mice *one square = 1″ (2·5cm)*

6 Owls and Pussy-cats (opposite)
Top and right : pussy-cats (lionesses). *Bottom and left :* owls.

The nose is a small, tightly stuffed ball of felt. Run a gathering thread around the edge of the felt, pull up to form a cup, insert the stuffing then finish pulling up and fasten off. Use an entirely separate thread to sew the nose to the tip of the body.

Finally, assemble the various parts of each eye. Glue or stitch them together then arrange them on the face and glue in place.

The apron strap for mother harvest mouse will have to be joined to make the correct length. Apart from that, the aprons are made in the same way. Make a narrow hem down both short sides and along one long side of the apron skirt. Gather the top edge of the skirt only slightly. Place the skirt in the centre of the strap with right sides of both together, and sew. Now fold strap over so that right sides of fabric are together. Sew each strap on either side of the skirt. Turn straps right side out through the opening by the gathers of the skirt. Now close this opening with a tiny slip stitch. Iron the apron before tying on to the harvest mouse.

Cut the cape from velvet, then draft a new pattern for the collar and lining by cutting the cape pattern in half along the collar/lining neck edge. Add a $\frac{1}{4}''$ (6 mm) seam allowance to both the collar and the lining on this neck edge. Join the lining to the collar with right sides facing, leaving a small opening in the centre for turning through. Now place right side of this new lining on the right side of the velvet cape and sew all the way round the edge. Turn cape through the opening in the neck edge of the lining. Slip stitch the opening. The completed cape is difficult to iron, so I would advise you to make sure that all the pieces are smooth before starting to sew and that you work carefully, avoiding any unnecessary creasing. Make a fastening at the front neck edge. Finally, roll the collar over, drape cape around the shoulders of mother harvest mouse, and fasten.

Further ideas for you to try

Design a waistcoat for the mice and you will have a father. Make the mice from gaily patterned cotton fabric. Line the ears with plain coloured felt or fabric and draft a pattern for arms by using those of the hippopotamus as a guide. There is no need to dress these.

9 The Owl and the Pussy-cat

'The owl and the pussy-cat went to sea
In a beautiful pea-green boat.
They took some honey, and plenty of money
Wrapped up in a five pound note.'

These are the opening lines to the well known nursery poem, although in this instance the owl is accompanied by a slightly larger jungle cat. The toys consist of a very simple body that relies on felt appliqué to provide the distinguishing features. By altering these features it is possible to make long or short-eared owls, snowy owls, and cats of all kinds. I have chosen a long-eared owl to accompany the lioness.

Owl

Most owls are nocturnal, sleeping by day and hunting by night. The wide eyes with the 'all knowing' look undoubtedly help to explain why owls are fictionally attributed with great powers of wisdom.

Materials:
a 9″ (23 cm) square of felt
¼ yd (23 cm) of 36″ (91 cm) wide fabric
yellow felt for beak
8 ozs (227 g) stuffing
black and white felt for eyes

Cutting:
Prepare pattern from the graph on page 68. Place base on folded paper as directed, in order to make a complete pattern. This makes an owl 8″ (20 cm) tall. Cut the body back, front, base, and wings from fabric. Cut the feet, ears, and face panel from the square of felt.

The fabric of the body is sewn on the wrong side while all the felt features are top stitched or glued to the body. Top stitching can be worked in several ways. You may choose to use your machine with either a straight stitch or a zig zag. On the other hand, felt features may be embroidered on to the body. Choose a contrasting coloured thread to highlight the appliqué.

Sew the face panel to body front, following the guide line marked on the pattern. Make each ear by placing two felt pieces together and top stitching the outer edge. Fold the ears in half and then baste them in position, just above the face panel, one on either side. They should lie directed inwards.

Sew the two beak pieces together round the curved edge only. Work tiny wisps of stuffing into the point of the beak, so that it is really firm. Centre the beak on the face panel, spreading the flaps out on either side. Hem these in place.

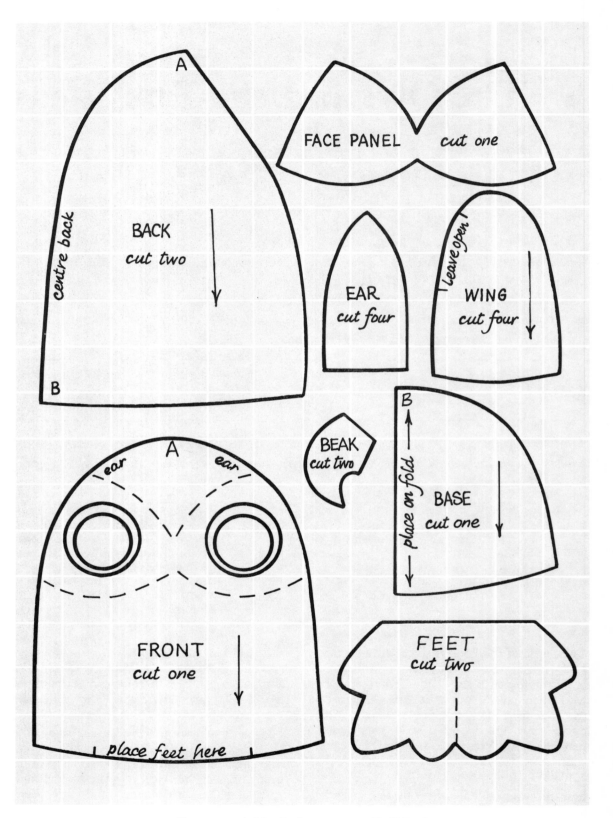

Pattern graph 15 Owl *one square = 1" (2·5cm)*

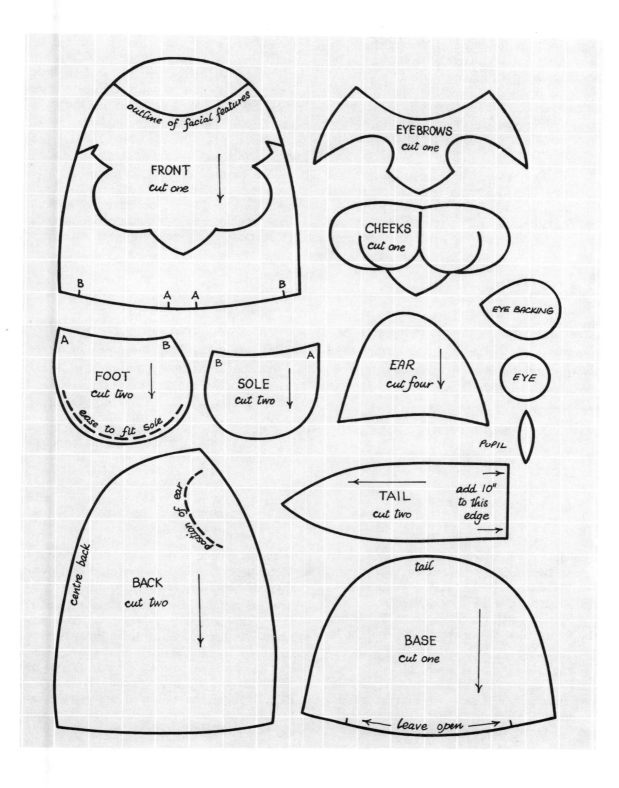

Pattern graph 16   Lioness *one square = 1″ (2·5cm)*

Top stitch the feet together around the outer curved edge. Mark a cleft between the feet by stitching along the line marked on the pattern. There is no need to slash the cleft. Stuff the feet lightly then baste them to the front body with the claws facing the ears. If you wish to hand sew the eyes to the face, then now is the time to do it.

Place right sides of back pieces together and sew the centre back seam. Insert the front and sew the side seams from the centre top to the base on either side. Insert base and sew around the curved edge, leaving the front edge open for stuffing. Turn body skin right side out and stuff the owl firmly. Close opening with ladder stitch. The feet will tend to drop down. This tendency can be counteracted by working a row of ladder stitching across the top of the feet drawing them up to the body front.

Glue the pupils to the eye whites and then glue the finished eyes to the face panel.

It only remains now to make the wings. Place two wing pieces together and sew on the wrong side. Turn right side out and lightly stuff. Close opening and sew wing to side of body. Make the second wing in the same way.

Lioness

Lions are family animals, living in large prides that contain several wives and children. They are essentially lazy cats, preferring to sleep the day away under the shade of a tree. In classical times there were lions in Greece, but nowadays they are found only in Africa and Southern Asia.

Materials: chocolate felt for eyebrows
tan felt for cheeks
white, yellow, and black felt for eyes
½ yd (46 cm) of 36″ or 48″ (91 cm or 122 cm) wide fabric
10 ozs (280 g) stuffing

Cutting: Prepare a set of patterns from the pattern graph, page 69. Add the extra length to the tail pattern. The lioness measures 9″ (23 cm) to the top of her ears. Cut the body from fabric, reversing the pattern when necessary to cut pairs of feet, ears and back pieces.

Assemble the felt facial features and start the lioness by attaching these to the body front. Work a mouth on the cheeks, using either a machined satin stitch or a hand worked chain stitch. Top stitch cheeks to body. Top stitch the upper edge of the eyebrows to the body.

Sew the pupil to the eye, then the eye to the eye backing. Now find the position for the eyes and glue them in place so that the lower edge lies over the cheeks and the upper and inner edges lie under the eyebrows. Finish attaching the eyebrows by sewing around eye and nose edge.

Run an easing thread along the edge of each foot. Place right sides of feet and soles together, pull on the easing thread until the edges fit together, then sew the entire outer curved edge. Turn feet right side out and lightly stuff. Place each foot to body front, matching each A to A and B to B respectively. Baste in position on the right side, check that they are even, then sew.

Sew the two backs together along the centre back seam. Insert body front and sew side seams from centre top to base. Place the two tail pieces together and sew on the wrong side, leaving short straight edge open. Turn tail right side out and baste to base. Position the base, tucking the tail well away from the machine, and sew. Turn body skin right side out and stuff firmly. Close the opening with ladder stitch.

Place each pair of ears together and sew around the outside edge on the wrong side. Turn through and fold in the raw edges. Close opening with ladder stitch, pulling up ever so slightly to gather the base. Sew ears to head.

Further ideas for you to try

Short-eared Owl Cut the ears in half and make the owl in the same way as already described.

Snowy Owl Use fur fabric for the body, but shave fur away from front before attaching face panel.

Lion Cover the upper part of the body with looped wool curls. Make them long enough to produce a thick, rich mane.

Tiger Appliqué black felt stripes over the surface.

Leopard Appliqué black spots and patches over body.

Pussy-cat Omit eyebrows and cut a smaller red nose. Work french knots and long, straight stitches on the cheeks to represent whiskers. Stuff the tail

10 Cloth Dolls

Dolls have played an important part in the lives of both children and adults, for it is quite likely that among the very first dolls were the religious symbols connected with superstitions and tribal rituals. They would have been made from natural materials near to hand, like bone, wood, stone, clay, skins, feathers, gourds, straw, and leaves. These same materials would also have been used in the home to make dolls for children, although very few examples of cloth dolls have survived the ravages of time and play.

The history of dolls includes the elaborate fashion dolls of the Middle Ages, pedlar dolls, national costume dolls, historical costume dolls, the dolls of the famous Nuremberg toy makers, as well as the doll derivatives like puppets, marionettes, and dolls' houses. The following patterns will introduce you to cloth doll construction, from which you can develop your own ideas.

Pocket Dolly

Pocket Dolly is a small cloth doll. She consists of a simple outline shape cut from a double layer of gingham and sewn around the edge; the doll is turned right side out through the head and stuffed. This type of doll was very popular at the beginning of the twentieth century when it was printed on strips of cotton and sold as a cloth cut out kit. The main drawback of the pattern unfortunately is the stiffness of the doll – the limbs cannot bend and she is difficult to dress. However, if the doll is kept small enough to fit in a pocket, she then makes a very personable toy. Since only a small amount of material is needed to clothe her, Pocket Dolly can even have a new set of clothes every time her owner has a new summer dress.

Materials: $\frac{1}{3}$ yd (30 cm) of 36″ (91 cm) wide gingham
4 ozs (112 g) stuffing
$\frac{1}{2}$ oz (13 g) double knitting (thick) wool
felt for eyes
6″ (15 cm) of 36″ (91 cm) wide cotton fabric
narrow elastic
lace trim or braid for dress

Cutting: Make patterns from the pattern graph. This makes a doll 10″ (25·5 cm) tall. Place body pattern on double layer of gingham and cut, but do not slash between legs until they have been stitched. Cut dress and pants from cotton fabric.

Place right sides of body together and machine around the edge and either side of the slash line for the legs, leaving an opening at the top of the head for turning the skin through. It is

72

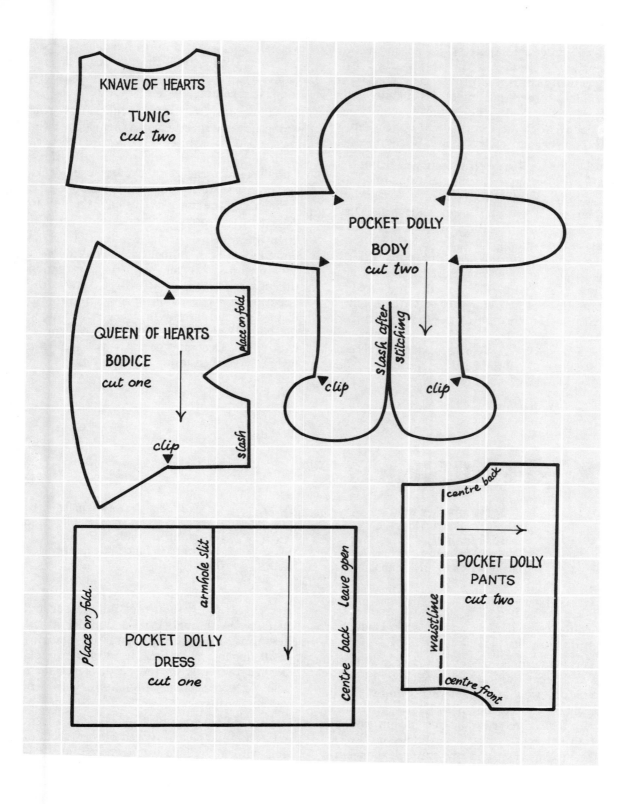

KNAVE OF HEARTS

TUNIC
cut two

POCKET DOLLY

BODY
cut two

slash after stitching

clip   *clip*

QUEEN OF HEARTS

BODICE
cut one

place on fold

clip   *slash*

armhole slit

POCKET DOLLY
DRESS
cut one

place on fold.

centre back   *leave open*

centre back

POCKET DOLLY
PANTS
cut two

waistline

centre front

Pattern graph 17   Pocket Dolly *one square = 1″ (2·5cm)*

73

as well to double stitch the doll as there is considerable tension on the seams when it is eventually stuffed. Clip into neck, underarm, and foot corners and angles. Slash between the legs. Turn right side out and stuff, commencing with the feet followed by legs, arms, body, neck, and lastly the head. Close opening.

Wind the wool into a hank and then cut it into 9″ (23 cm) lengths. Tie the resulting bundle of wool in the middle with one of the strands and then sew this wig to the top of the head. Don't worry about trimming it until you have finished working the face. Cut two small circles of felt for the eyes, then stitch them in position with two straight stitches, forming a four point star. The mouth is worked in buttonhole stitch with red cotton; imagine a clock in the position of the mouth and work buttonhole stitches so that they cover one o'clock to eleven o'clock. Fasten the threads off on the top of the head, under the wig. The wig can now be glued to the head, so covering the thread ends and the stuffing opening. Groom the hair, trimming the ends, cutting a fringe (bangs), and adding a bow.

Sew the centre front seam of the pants on the wrong side and make a narrow hem around the lower edge of each leg. Sew the centre back seam and the under leg seam on both sides. Clip the crotch where all the seams meet. Make a hem at the waist and thread narrow elastic through it. Measure pants against the doll to determine the correct length.

With the dress, turn under and machine the raw edges of both armhole slits. Fold the neck edge over by $\frac{1}{4}$″ (6 mm) and run a gathering thread from back edge across the front to the opposite back edge. Pull up gathering thread to fit neck and fasten off. Make a hem along the bottom edge of the dress and neaten the back edges. Decorate the dress with lace trim or braid and then fasten it to the dolly.

Knave of Hearts

Materials: $\frac{1}{2}$ oz (13 g) yellow wool for hair
24″ (61 cm) red ric rac
red felt for heart
a 9″ (23 cm) square of blue felt
60″ (152·5 cm) red ribbon $1\frac{1}{2}$″ (4 cm) wide

Cutting: Cut the body from gingham as described for Pocket Dolly. Make a pattern of the tunic from the graph and cut from blue felt. Cut the heart from red felt.

Make the body and face of the Knave by following instructions given for Pocket Dolly, but omit the mouth.

The hair can be made in two very different ways, depending on your preference. Firstly, wind the wool over a ruler, covering it evenly along its length. Lower machine needle and, with foot raised, ease the first inch of wool off the ruler and lay it against the needle. Lower the machine foot and sew through the centre of the wool. Ease more wool up the ruler and off the end under the machine foot and continue to sew in this way until all the wool is removed from the ruler. The second method of making curls consists of winding the wool over an 18″ (46 cm) strip of thick paper and then sewing through wool and paper at the same time. Tear the paper away by removing small amounts at a time from side to side. Arrange the curls on the head, laying them close together so that all stitching is hidden. Backstitch into place.

Sew the ric rac around the edge of both front and back tunic pieces. Attach heart to front of tunic with buttonhole stitch worked in yellow thread. Lay both tunic pieces against the doll and catch at the shoulders and under each arm. Fold the ribbon in half, lengthways, and gather the folded edge. Draw up to form a ruff and stitch securely to neck edge of the tunic.

Queen of Hearts

It seems only natural that the Queen should accompany the Knave – so here she is.

Materials: ½ oz (13 g) yellow double knitting (thick) wool
gold braid for crown
pearl beads for crown
⅓ yd (30 cm) of 36″ (91 cm) wide blue cotton or poplin
44″ (112 cm) lace 1″ (2·5 cm) wide
44″ (112 cm) red ribbon 1½″ (4 cm) wide
red ric rac, gold braid, gold ric rac and red felt to decorate the dress

Cutting: Cut the body from gingham as described for Pocket Dolly. Cut dress and petticoat from blue cotton. Dress skirt measures 21″ (53 cm)×5½″ (14 cm) and petticoat measures 21″ (53 cm)×4½″ (11 cm). Cut heart shapes from red felt. The red ribbon is for the inner sleeves. All other trimmings are for the dress.

Make the body and face of the Queen by following instructions given for Pocket Dolly. Work a few, close rows of stem stitch for the mouth. Do this with red thread.

Make a cardboard template for the hair. It should measure 8″ (20 cm)×3″ (7·5 cm). Wind the wool over the template, covering it evenly. Carefully remove the loops from the card, and then sew through the centre so that the loops are on either side of a central parting. Arrange the wig on top of the head with fullness at the crown. Attach to the head by sewing through the parting with matching thread. Reserve a generous cluster of loops at the centre back end of the parting. These are used to make a bun on the very top of the head. Collect together all the other loops and stitch them down at the nape of the neck. Fold the bun loops in half and then stitch to the top of the head (see Figure 20, below).

Use a small length of gold braid to make the crown. Decorate it with pearls or other rich-looking beads. Sew the crown to the head so that it encircles the bun.

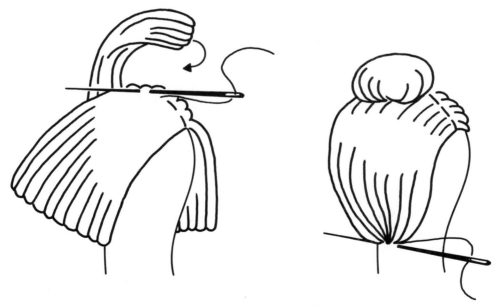

Figure 20 Construction of hair for the Queen of Hearts

75

Make a narrow hem on the lower edge of the petticoat and attach two rows of lace to hide the hem. Close the centre back seam. Gather the waist edge and pull up on the gathers until the petticoat fits the waist. Sew petticoat to the body.

The false inner sleeves are made by gathering half the red ribbon for each arm. Sew them to the arm at the elbow level so that the ribbon will just project beyond the dress sleeve edge.

Slash a centre back opening on one half of the combined bodice and sleeve piece of material. Hem both sleeve edges and decorate with ric rac or braid. Neaten the neck edge with a narrow bias strip. Sew both underarm sleeve seams and then clip at right angles where seam ends. Make a narrow hem on the lower edge of the skirt. Decorate with braid and hearts. Gather the waist edge and fit against the bodice to determine the correct width. Sew skirt to bodice.

Cut a large felt heart to cover the front of the bodice. Use a yellow thread and buttonhole stitch to attach it to the dress. Work some form of embroidery or decoration on the heart. I used alternating rows of gold ric rac and braid.

Iron dress if necessary, then put on to the Queen. Sew the back opening to the doll as far as the waist then ladder stitch both sides of the skirt together.

Basic Dolly

Although still simple in design, Basic Dolly has the advantage of moveable arms and legs. This movement is made possible by hinges at the position of the shoulders and hips, and the doll is thus described as being single-hinged. This distinguishes it from a double-hinged doll which has additional hinges at the elbow and knee positions. The head is cut separately from the body, eliminating the perennial problem of a wobbly neck. Such 'wobbliness' is the result of the stuffing disappearing from the neck as it becomes compacted in head and body. The pattern for Basic Dolly includes three different sets of clothes. Firstly there is the Elf with his outfit of felt tunic and hat. The tunic is easily made as it is stitched permanently on to the body, and felt requires no hemming. Katherine, as the name implies, is Basic Dolly dressed as a little girl in smock and knickers. Karl has long denim trousers and a shirt. Instructions for making different hair styles and facial features are given with each doll.

Materials: ½ yd (46 cm) of flesh-coloured or off-white cotton, poplin, crash, calico, or gingham
(1 yd (91 cm) makes three dolls)
6 ozs (170 g) stuffing
double knitting (thick) wool, embroidery thread and felts – refer to the doll that you are making for quantities needed

Cutting: Make a pattern of the body from the pattern graph. This makes a doll 16″ (40·5 cm) tall. Cut out all pieces, remembering to make pairs of legs, arms, and head pieces. There should be 13 pieces in all.

Place pairs of arms together with right sides facing and sew, leaving top edge open. Place pairs of legs together in the same way and sew, again leaving top edge open. Trim hand and foot curves, then turn the limbs right side out and stuff each one firmly to within one inch of the top opening. Hold stuffing away from the opening, using either a pin or large tacking stitches, until limbs are stitched to the body. Position arms in the arm slits and baste. Sew. Match centre fronts and shoulders of the body and sew on the wrong side. Make a double row of gathering stitches along the lower back curved edge. Pull up gathers to fit lower front

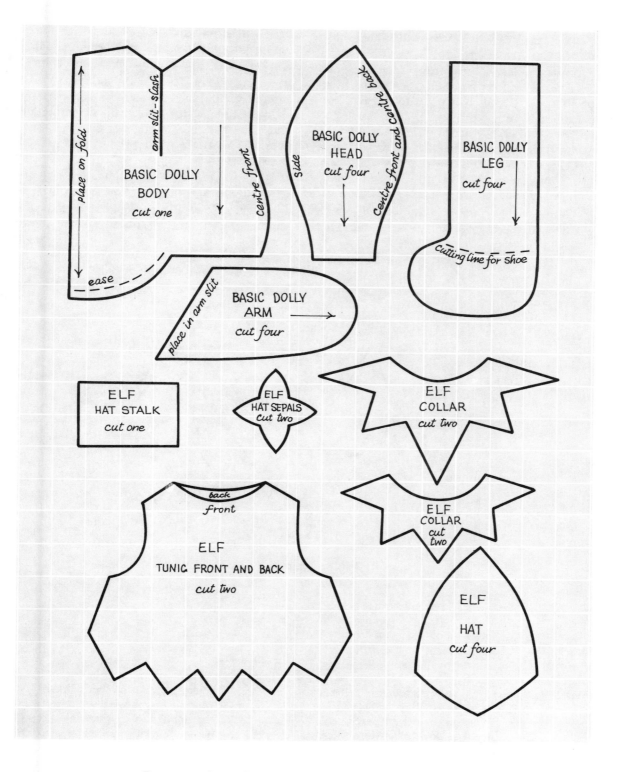

Pattern graph 18 Basic Dolly and Elf *one square = 1″ (2·5cm)*

edge (see Figure 21, below). Turn body right side out.

Press tops of legs together to bring the respective seams into centre front and centre back position, so that the toes point forwards. Now place legs into lower edge of body and sew securely, either by machining on the surface or by using ladder stitch for hidden sewing (see Figure 21). Stuff body firmly and close neck by gathering up and fastening off. Remove pins or tacking stitches from the tops of the limbs.

Place head pieces together in pairs and sew both centre front and centre back seams on the wrong side. Sew front to back head, matching seams at the crown and leaving neck open.

Trim curves and turn right side out. Stuff carefully, moulding the head into a pleasant shape. Close neck opening by gathering up and turning in the raw edges at the same time. Work a few stitches across the gathers to hold the stuffing in position.

Position head on shoulders and stitch to body with very strong thread. Work twice around the neck, at least, using a separate thread each time as precaution against head working loose.

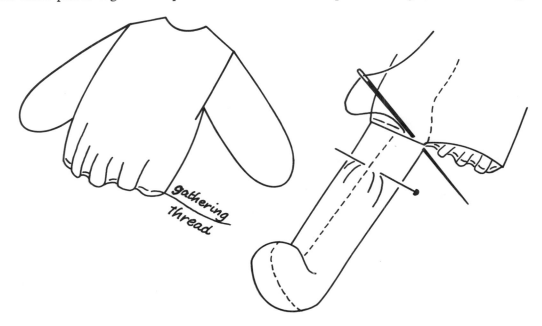

Figure 21 Construction of body, Basic Dolly

Elf

Materials: ¼ yd (23 cm) green fabric for body
flesh-coloured fabric for head (¼ yd (23 cm) makes several heads)
1 oz (28 g) double knitting (thick) wool
small pieces of felt for eyes
embroidery thread for mouth
12″ (30·5 cm) × 18″ (46 cm) green felt
a 9″ (23 cm) square of yellow felt
a 9″ (23 cm) square of gold felt

Make body as for Basic Dolly.

Cutting: Make patterns of the clothes from the graph, page 77. Cut tunic, hat and hat stalk from green felt, 7 pieces in all. Cut large collar and one set of sepals from yellow felt, 3 pieces, and small collar and set of sepals from gold felt, again 3 pieces in all.

To make the wig, wind the wool into a hank and then cut into 10″ (25·5 cm) lengths. Spread the lengths out until they are 6″ (15 cm) wide and then machine through the middle. If you are hand stitching the wig, then backstitch the wool to a length of tape. This makes a centre parting. Lay the wig on the head and sew in place through the parting. Work the face first, before finishing off the wig.

Cut three small circles of felt for each eye. I used orange for the largest, followed by gold and then black for the pupil. Stitch in place with a four point star using the same coloured reddish thread used for the mouth. The mouth is a gentle curve worked in stem stitch. The ends of the threads can be fastened off under the wig. Now spread glue under the wig and press the wool against the head. Trim the ends and cut a fringe. You will find this easier to do after making the hat and trying it on for size.

Sew the side seams of the tunic. These need only be ⅛″ (3 mm) wide. Turn right side out and slip tunic on to the body. Fasten the shoulder seams together. Lay collar pieces around the neck with the smaller collar uppermost and fasten to the Elf on the shoulders.

Place hat sections together in pairs and sew. Then put the two halves together and sew. Turn right side out. Roll the stalk tightly and close the edge with a small slip stitch. Place both sets of sepals together so that they alternate and sew stalk to the centre and then through to the centre of the hat. Put hat on Elf and finish trimming the hair.

Karl

Materials: ½ yd (46 cm) of flesh-coloured fabric for body
2 ozs (56 g) double double (rug) wool
small pieces of felt for eyes
⅓ yd (30 cm) of denim
elastic
¼ yd (23 cm) patterned cotton fabric
3 small buttons
3 small press studs (snappers)

Cutting: Make body as for Basic Dolly. Prepare pattern of clothes from the graph on page 80. Place trousers on folded paper to make a complete pattern, taking care to raise the back and lower the front waist edge. Cut trousers from denim and the shirt from the patterned cotton.

Make the wig by winding the wool into a 30″ (76 cm) hank and then cutting it into 10″ (25·5 cm) lengths. Reserve a few strands of wool. Use one to tie all the lengths together, just off centre. This represents a side parting. Lay wig on head and sew securely to the doll with remaining strands of wool. Make the face before gluing the wig down.

Work mouth in stranded cotton and add a few freckles of french knots to each cheek. The eyes are two circles of light brown felt held in place by a four point star worked in pale blue thread. Now glue the hair down and trim by cutting it in layers and making a small fringe (bangs) on the forehead.

Place both trouser pieces together with right sides facing and sew the centre front seam.

Make a narrow hem on the bottom of each trouser leg. Clip crotch. Sew the centre back and under leg seams on the wrong side. Clip crotch. Turn trousers right side out, fold to find the front of each leg and press with an iron. Stitch a permanent crease line, ⅛″ (3 mm) from the folded edge.

Make a hem at the waist and thread with narrow elastic. You might like to make a belt using felt or leather and a shoe or watch strap buckle.

The shirt is made by placing fronts and back together with right sides facing and sewing the upper arm and shoulder seam on both sides. Make a narrow hem at both sleeve edges then sew both underarm and side seams. Clip underarm. Neaten front facing edge and turn

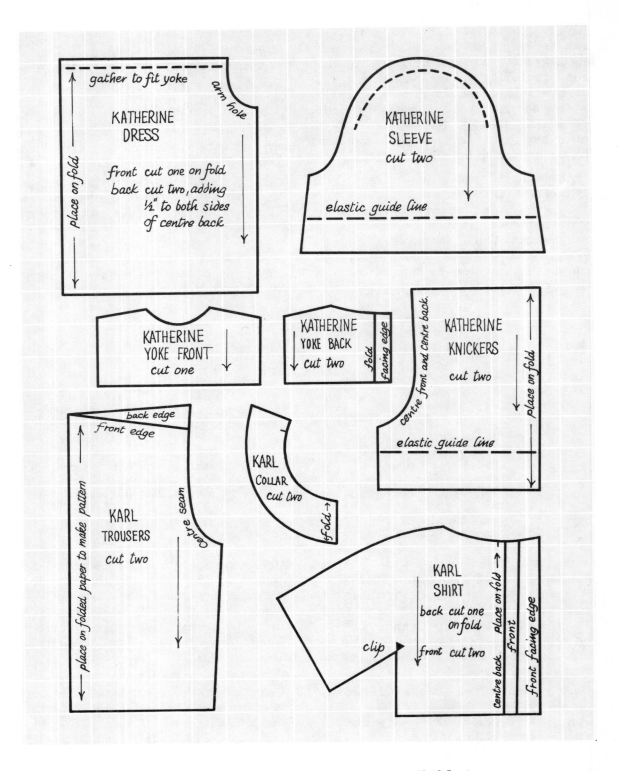

Pattern graph 19   Katherine and Karl *one square = 1" (2·5cm)*

7 Cloth Dolls (including Susan Jane) (opposite)
Top, from left to right : Pocket Dolly, Elf. *Middle :* Susan Jane, Katherine, Karl. *Bottom :* Queen of
Hearts, Knave of Hearts.

the allowance under. Hem bottom edge of shirt. Check the shirt for size, especially the neck, by trying on Karl. Remove shirt and give it a good pressing before proceeding.

Sew both collar pieces together around the outer curved and short straight edge, on the wrong side. Trim excess material away from seam and clip the front corners off. Turn collar right side out and press. Baste open edges together on the inner curve. Match centre back of collar to shirt, on the right side, and sew. Neaten the inside neck edge with a small bias strip hemmed in place.

Sew buttons to front of shirt and attach press studs under each button.

If wanted, you can make shoes by using the foot pattern. Cut these from felt and trim the edges so that there is only $\frac{1}{8}''$ (3 mm) seam.

Katherine

Materials: $\frac{1}{2}$ yd (46 cm) of flesh-coloured fabric for body
2 ozs (56 g) double double (rug) wool
felt for eyes
embroidery thread for face
$\frac{1}{2}$ yd (46 cm) of gingham
narrow elastic
54″ (136 cm) broderie anglaise (eyelet edging)
felt for shoes
2 or three small press studs (snappers)

Cutting: Make body as for Basic Dolly.
Make patterns of the clothes from the pattern graph. Place knickers and dress on folded paper to make complete patterns. Cut all pieces from gingham.

Make the wig by winding the wool into a 44″ (112 cm) hank. Do this around a couple of chairs and you will find it much easier. Cut the loops at both ends of the hank. Remove 20 strands in all, 14 to make the fringe and 6 for stitching the wig to the head and tying off the plaits. Cut the fringe strands in half, twice, and machine across the middle of these short lengths. Place stitched line across forehead, level with front edge of the fringe line. Sew fringe to head. Now anchor down the cut ends on the top of the head, either by gluing or stitching.

Spread the bulk of the hank out to a width of 5″ (12.5 cm) and machine across the middle to make a centre parting. Lay on head so that the front edge hides the raw edges of the fringe. Sew in place using a strand of the same coloured wool. Divide hair on either side and make two plaits (braids). Tie ends with same coloured wool. Catch plaits to side of head after spreading glue under the bulk of the wig. Trim the ends of the plaits neatly, and tie on a ribbon if needed.

Cut two blue felt circles for the eyes and stitch them to the face with an eight point star. Embroider a mouth in stem stitch with red thread and make cheeks of circular rows of running stitch in pink thread.

Start by making the knickers. Place both pieces together with right sides facing and sew the centre front seam. Neaten the bottom edge of each leg with a narrow hem and a row of broderie anglaise. Stitch narrow elastic to the inside of each leg, stretching it as you go. The zig zagger of a machine is ideal for this purpose. Now sew the centre back seam and the under leg seams. Clip the crotch.

Make a narrow hem at the waist edge and thread with elastic. Press the knickers and then put them on the dolly. Never make the elastic so tight that it is both difficult for a child to dress and undress the doll and constricting on the stuffing inside the body.

Now you are ready to make the little smock. Place the front and back yoke pieces together with right sides facing and sew the shoulder seams. Gather the top of both dress pieces to fit the corresponding yoke edges. Baste and sew dress to yoke. Gather the head of each sleeve and baste to arm hole edge of dress. Arrange the fullness evenly and sew on the wrong side.

Make narrow hems on the sleeve edges and attach a row of broderie anglaise. Work a row of elastic, following the guide line marked on the pattern. Sew underarm and side seams of dress in one continuous movement. Clip underarm corner.

Neaten the back facing edge and make a hem on the bottom of the dress. Check the neck for size by trying dress on Katherine. Cut away if necessary. Neaten the neck edge with a strip of bias. Sew a few press studs to the back opening. Decorate the dress with broderie anglaise, buttons and bows. I gathered a short length, then folded the two sides together, stitched it to the front of the dress and added a few red buttons.

Shoes can be made by cutting felt pieces to correspond with the foot pattern. Cut a thin strap and sew to either side of shoes, or use buttons and press studs if you want the shoes to be removable.

With fair hair and plaits, Katherine could equally well be Goldilocks. Make a little red cape for her and you have Red Riding Hood. The variations are endless and you should have fun dressing her as you please. Make the legs longer and you have the very modern dolly shape you can dress with stockings and boots.

11 A Very Special Rag Doll

Dressing dolls in authentic historical costume can involve you in many hours of pleasurable research, either through books or visits to museums. Since mediaeval times, it has been a European custom to send fashion dolls between the Royal courts. These dolls were often life-size, like their modern sisters in the main street windows of today. Many examples of these dolls and smaller ones have survived to provide us with intimate detail of costume.

Finding suitable fabrics is often a problem, for you should avoid using any synthetic material, lace, or trimmings. Another difficulty is that some fabrics drape well enough on us, but when reduced to doll-sized proportions are quite useless. Fabrics that are most suitable are silk, satin, velvet, wool, brocade, linen, and cotton. Remember too that sewing machines and elastic were unknown before the middle of the nineteenth century. Clothes made before this time would have had many more tucks, pleats, gathers, and plackets. Tapes were also used to tie on undergarments. Watch these points if you are making exhibition dolls.

Susan Jane, a Costume Doll

In making Susan Jane, I have aimed for a costume of the mid eighteenth century. At the same time, I have designed the clothes so that a child can dress and undress the doll, for surely this is the purpose of the toy. This means that elastic has been used, although not where it would be too obvious. Seams have been sewn on a machine for extra strength and there are a few press studs on the petticoat. Quilted underskirts were very popular at this time, but would be too heavy on a doll, so I have used quilting for the front panel only and sewn it to a taffeta foundation. Another feature of costumes at this time was the rich decoration. Lace, frills, ribbons, bows, jewels, and flounces were all the rage (see Figure 23, page 89).

The pattern for the body is more sophisticated than that of the basic doll. She has many more pieces in the head to make cheeks. The hands and feet are shaped and there is an interesting surface hinge at the top of the legs which allows her to sit.

Materials: ½ yd (46 cm) of 56″ (141 cm) wide calico
1½ lbs (681 g) stuffing
8 ozs (227 g) double double (rug) wool for hair
small pieces of felt for facial features

Cutting: Cut two each of legs, upper feet, soles, bodies. Cut one only head front and head back. Cut two pairs of arms, head side fronts, and head side backs. Graph is on page 85.

Work throughout on the wrong side of the calico unless told otherwise. For all hand stitching, use double linen thread.

Assemble the head first. Make the front half by sewing a side front to each side of the centre front. Then make the back half by sewing a side back to each side of the centre back. Now sew the front and back heads together, being careful to match the seams on the crown. Leave the neck open. If you prefer to embroider a face, then now is the time to do it. Trim the seams and clip the cheek curves. Turn head right side out and stuff, paying particular attention to the cheeks. Close the neck opening by working a gathering thread around the edge and drawing up to fasten off. Put head aside.

Prepare arms by placing each pair together and sewing around the outside. Leave an opening for turning. Slash between thumb and hand and trim the curves. Turn arm right side out, stuff and close the opening.

Sew each foot upper to sole, from A to B. Place this foot section to lower edge of leg, matching C, A, and D, and sew. Run a gathering thread around the toe edge and ease up to fit the sole. Fold legs in half lengthways and sew around foot and inside leg seams. Leave the top open for turning. Clip any seams that may be trapped at the ankles, although if you break stitching at ankle by raising machine foot, and move over the seam, this would not be necessary. Turn legs right side out.

Stuff feet and ankles firmly before stuffing the leg. Work the stuffing in evenly so that the legs are smooth and not knobbly. Don't work beyond the stuffing line marked on the pattern. Now topstitch this upper region of the legs by following the guide lines marked on the pattern. This flattened area acts as a fabric hinge and allows mobility at the hips for sitting.

Place both body pieces together and sew from neck edge down each side to the hip edge. Clip across the shoulder corner and turn body right side out. Now place tops of legs against the lower edge of the front, matching raw edges by turning the legs forward to lie either side of the neck. Sew them together twice. Turn under seam allowance on the back edge and ladder stitch it to the front and tops of legs.

Stuff body through the neck opening. Close the neck edge by slightly gathering up and working some stitches across the opening to hold the stuffing in. Place head on shoulders and ladder stitch the two together, twice at least, with separate threads each time.

Poke in the top edge of the shoulders to form a small projection over a socket. The top of the arms will just fit into this recess. Ladder stitch and oversew arms to body, securely, but still allowing freedom of movement.

To make the hair, you will need two 4 oz balls of thick wool. Take one of the balls of wool and wind it into a 34" (86 cm) hank. Cut this into two smaller hanks, 16" (40·5 cm) and 18" (46 cm). The former will make the front hair while the latter will make the back hair. Wind the second ball of wool into a 48" (122 cm) hank. Remove 34 strands from this hank and plait them together into a long braid. The remaining strands of the hank are used to make ringlets.

To make ringlets, divide the remainder of the hank into four equal bunches. Take one bunch, hold both ends firmly and twist the wool. You will need a helping pair of hands to do this. Continue twisting the wool until you feel it ready to coil upon itself. Without letting go of the ends, fold the wool in half and pull apart. Now let go of the looped ends and it should spring into two ringlets. Pull them into equal lengths and catch them together at the top by tying to the cut ends of the wool. Make three more pairs of ringlets in the same way. Sew two pairs of ringlets to each side of the head (see Figure 22, page 78).

Take the hank for the front hair and machine across the cut ends at one end only. It should be about 3" (7.5 cm) wide. Sew to the crown of the head, between the side fronts. Now lift up the top half of this hair and pull to one side of the face. Lay part of the hair in front of the ringlets and the remainder behind the ringlets. Pull down firmly to the neck beneath the ringlets and catch securely in place. Fold the ends back up towards the crown and sew down neatly. Take the remaining lower half of the front hair, pull to the other side of the face, lay on either side of the ringlets, and proceed as already described.

Sew across the ends of the hank for the back

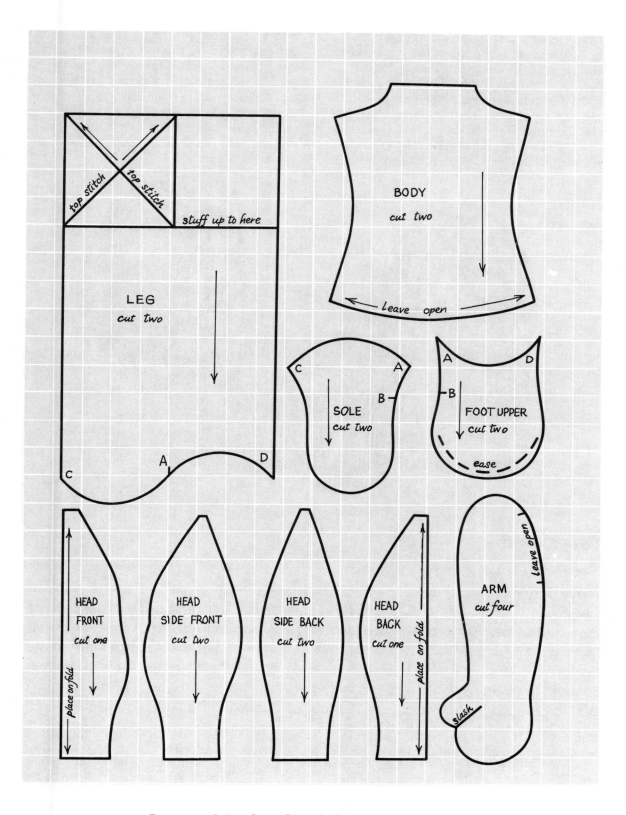

Pattern graph 20   Susan Jane—body *one square = 1″ (2·5cm)*

hair. Lay on top of head next to the front hair and catch in place. Pull down to neck, covering any ends of the front hair that might be exposed, catch in place with large holding stitches and fold back up towards the crown. Tie all the ends together in a tight bunch, fold under and catch down to the crown. Try to arrange it so that the fold covers the beginnings of the front and back hair. I have hidden the join with a long plait although a large bow would do equally well. If you use a plait, then lay it across the join and down both sides of the head. Catch the ends together at the neck, tucking in any loose wool under the back hair. Cut felt shapes for the eyes and mouth. The eyebrows are stitched to the top edge of the eye with buttonhole stitch and then the complete unit is stuck to the face.

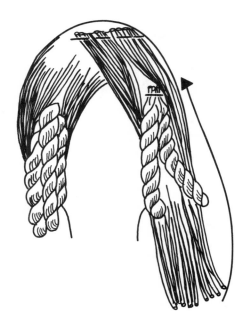

Figure 22 Construction of hair for Susan Jane

UNDERWEAR

Susan Jane's underwear consists of a pair of long pantaloons and full length petticoat (see Figure 23, page 89). Both garments are made from white cotton and are trimmed with broderie anglaise. Exquisitely made underwear would have narrow french seams. To make these, you first sew the seam on the right side then turn the garment through to the wrong side and sew the seam again. All the raw edges are now completely enclosed. Decide whether you wish to make french seams or not, and work accordingly.

Materials: 1 yd (91 cm) of 36″ (91 cm) wide white cotton
4 yds (366 cm) broderie anglaise (eyelet edging)
narrow elastic
2 press studs (snappers)

Cutting: Prepare patterns from the pattern graph. The bodice back and front are combined, so follow cutting lines carefully to distinguish between the two when making patterns. Cut fabric according to the pattern layout (see Figure 24, page 89).

86

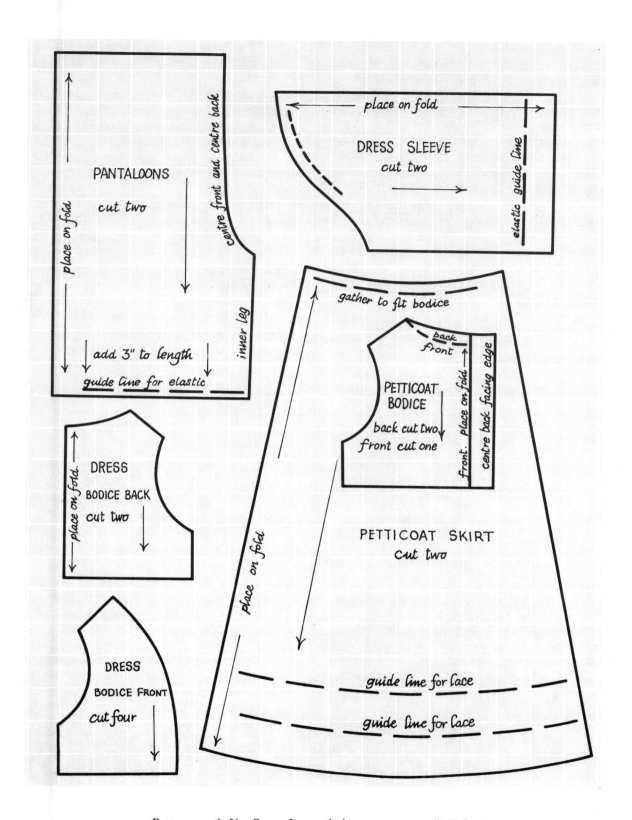

PANTALOONS

cut two

place on fold

centre front and centre back

inner leg

add 3" to length

guide line for elastic

place on fold

DRESS SLEEVE

cut two

elastic guide line

DRESS

BODICE BACK

cut two

place on fold.

DRESS

BODICE FRONT

cut four

gather to fit bodice

back

Front

PETTICOAT
BODICE

back cut two

front cut one

Front. place on fold

centre back facing edge

PETTICOAT SKIRT

cut two

place on fold

guide line for lace

guide line for lace

Pattern graph 21   Susan Jane—clothes *one square = 1" (2·5cm)*

Make the pantaloons first. Place both pieces together with right sides facing and sew the centre front seam. Hem the lower leg edges and trim with a row of broderie anglaise. Attach narrow elastic to legs, following guide lines on the pattern. Now sew the centre back seam and the inside leg seams. Clip the crotch. Turn pantaloons right side out and press. Make a hem at the waist and thread with elastic. Try against body to determine the correct width.

Now you are ready to make the petticoat. Place both skirt sections together and sew french seams down the sides. Make a small hem around the lower edge and decorate with two rows of broderie anglaise, following the guide lines on the pattern. Press the skirt, now, before gathering.

Fold skirt in half lengthways to find centre back at the waist edge, then slash an opening to form the lower half of the petticoat opening. Turn under raw edges of the slash and hem. Gather the waist edge and have it ready to fit against the bodice.

Sew bodice pieces together along both shoulder seams. Neaten the armhole edges by hemming or sewing on a bias strip. Do the same for the neck edge. Sew side seams under the arms. Lay skirt against bodice, spread fullness evenly and adjust the gathers as necessary to fit. Place right sides together and sew.

Finish the petticoat by attaching two press studs on the back opening. Put petticoat on doll. Authentic costumes of this period would have been fastened with tapes. Being cotton, you can starch it for more body, or you could as an alternative cut a vilene or organdy skirt. Use the petticoat pattern but trim it smaller so that there is no need to gather.

UNDERSKIRT

These often took the form of quilted petticoats, usually cream or fawn in colour. The patterns of the fabric were so beautiful that many ladies buttoned back their overskirts to expose a front view of the underskirt.

Materials: $\frac{2}{3}$ yd (61 cm) of 36″ (91 cm) wide fawn taffeta
24″ (61 cm) × 9″ (23 cm) brocade or quilting for the front panel
2 yds (182 cm) of wide lace
waist length of elastic
white tape
2 press studs (snappers)

Cutting: Make a pattern by following the measurements given in Figure 25, page 91, and cut one front panel from the brocade. Fold taffeta and cut the selvedge edge to match the angle of the front panel.

Place shaped sides of taffeta against the front panel, right sides facing, and sew. Leave an opening at the waist edge on both sides. This is necessary if the underskirt is to be removed easily. Make a hem along the lower edge, using cross stitch for the brocade. Lay the lace over the taffeta and sew a double row along the hem edge.

Make a hem at the waist of the taffeta and thread with elastic. Fold under raw edges on all sides of the front panel above the waist and hem. Sew a tape to each side of the top. This must be long enough to pass around the neck and tie in a bow. Close the waist openings between taffeta and brocade on each side of the waist with a press stud (see Figure 23).

OVERSKIRT

The dresses of the early eighteenth century were fashioned around rather formidable corsets and hoops, the hoops being used to hold heavy brocades and damasks in place. By the middle of the century, much of this formality was disappearing. Softer fabrics were being used, decorated with lace and trimmings. Frills were fashionable at the elbows, and skirts were being looped up at the back to make a puffed 'polonaise' style.

Figure 23 Clothes for Susan Jane, consisting of pantaloons, petticoat, underskirt, and overskirt

Materials: 1 yd (91 cm) of 44″ (112 cm) wide shot taffeta or other suitable fabric
2 yds (182 cm) lace for sleeves
3 yds (274 cm) thin gold cord
elastic to fit wrists
6 small pearl, beaded buttons
1 or more press studs (snappers)

Make the skirt of the dress first. Fold both the selvedges under to the wrong side to make a hem 1½″ (4 cm) wide. Gather one long edge to be the waist. Leave the final adjustment of width until you have the bodice to measure it against.

Cutting: Make patterns of the bodice and sleeve from the pattern graph. Cut a double set of bodice pieces to make a self lining. The skirt is an oblong measuring 20″ (51 cm) × 44″ (112 cm) wide. Do not remove the selvedge as this can be used on the front facing edge. Graph is on page 87.

Take one set of bodice pieces and sew them together on the wrong side at the shoulders. Gather the head of each sleeve and baste, then sew to armhole edges. Make a narrow hem at the wrist of each sleeve to act as an elastic casing. Sew several rows of lace to the edge of

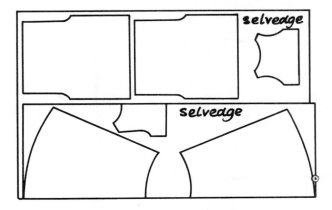

Figure 24 Layout for the underwear

89

each sleeve before inserting the elastic. Pull up so that the sleeve fits over the hand easily when dressing and undressing. Sew underarm sleeve seam and side seam of the bodice on both sides. Clip the underarm corner.

Make a lining for the bodice by using the duplicate set of bodice pieces. First, sew them together at the shoulders on the wrong side. Then lay the lining against the bodice proper, with right sides facing, and sew from the waist edge around the neck and down to the waist on the opposite side. Sew side seams of bodice lining. Now fold under raw edges of armholes and slip stitch both bodices together on the sleeve seam.

Baste skirt to waist edge of bodice, matching right sides. Adjust gathers evenly and sew. Sew again for extra strength. Fold under raw edge of bodice lining and hem along the machine line of the bodice and skirt. Turn up the hem of the skirt and sew.

Decorate the dress according to the type of fabric that you have used. I used a narrow gold cord to frame the front opening, waist and hem (see Figure 23, page 89). Make a fastening at the waist edge. This could be as simple as a couple of press studs on either side of the skirt or it could be more elaborate and therefore decorative. Susan Jane has a small frogging fastener, made from the cord used to frame the skirt. Lay the cord according to Figure 26, below. Do this over a padded board so that you can pin the loops down and hold them fast until they are stitched. Sew all loops securely on the side facing you. This becomes the wrong side of the finished frog.

Sew a press stud to one side. Remove frog from the board and turn over to right side. Check that all loops are secure, then sew a pearl bead in the centre of each loop. Do this by weaving your thread backwards and forwards across the loop. The frog is now ready to sew to the overskirt. Sew the other half of the press stud to the waist edge of the overskirt. Dress the doll and fasten.

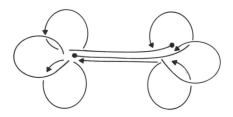

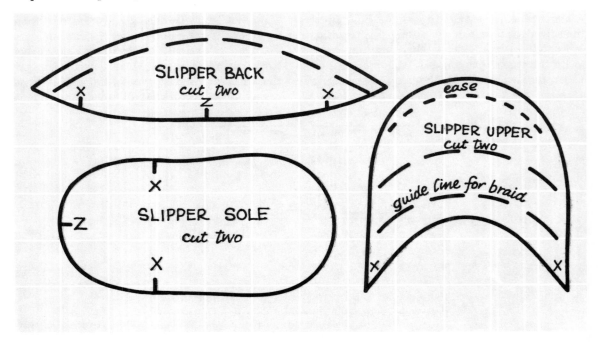

Pattern graph 22   Susan Jane—slippers *one square = 1″ (2·5cm)*

90

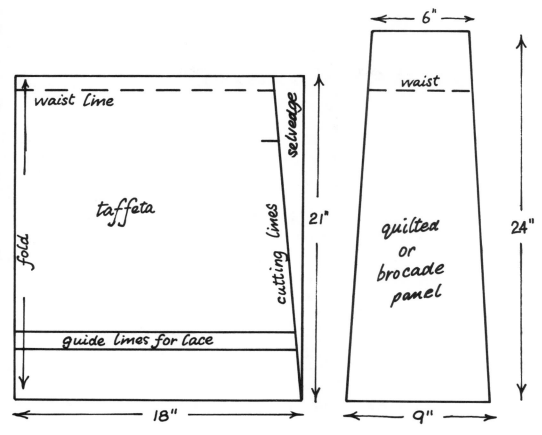

Figure 25 Pattern diagram for the underskirt

SLIPPERS

Materials: 2 pieces of felt 9″ (23 cm) square
            2 yds (182 cm) gold braid

Cutting: Prepare patterns from the pattern graph. Cut two pieces of each part. The slippers are identical, there being no right and left foot on the doll.

Sew braid to the back and upper pieces of both slippers. Place right sides of back and sole together, matching both Xs and Z. Sew. Ease the toe edge of the upper portion so that it fits the sole. Again match the Xs on the right side and sew. Turn slipper right side out. Sew braid around the edge to cover the sole seam. Place slipper on a foot and finish the other slipper in the same way.

12　Novelty Dolls

Many obvious examples spring to mind when thinking of novelty dolls. There are the old favourites like peg dolls, pedlar dolls, pipe cleaner miniatures, jesters and their folly dollies, musical dolls, baby buntings, and upside down dolls. Then there are all the more recent developments like trendy teenagers dressed in the latest 'gear', bean babies for posing, dolls from fiction and television like the Little Women *series and* Florence, *dolls depicting national costume from every country likely to have tourists, and of course mascot dolls. A few examples of these dolls are given here to start you on your way. If you find that doll making is your* forte *then there is a wealth of literature available covering many aspects of the craft.*

Jotho the Clown

Clowns have a very long history of being entertainers. In mediaeval days, they were the jesters, travelling from court to court. Then there was the Auguste, a character said to have been originated by Tom Belling during a performance in 1889. White faced clowns with oversized costumes and performances of 'clowning about' with water and cars are all developments of the present century.

This is a very simple pattern with potential for many modifications. The body consists of two long tubes, folded to make arms and legs. A head is sewn to the shoulders.

Materials:
$\frac{1}{4}$ yd (23 cm) of 48" (122 cm) wide fabric
$\frac{1}{4}$ yd (23 cm) skin-coloured fabric
a 9" (23 cm) square of felt for feet
felt for eyes and nose
2 oz (56 g) ball of wool
$\frac{1}{4}$ yd (23 cm) fabric for bow
1 lb (454 g) stuffing

Cutting:
Prepare patterns from the pattern graph. When finished, Jotho is 22" (56 cm) tall. Cut the body tubes from 48" (122 cm) fabric, remembering to reverse the pattern so that you have two pairs. Do not slash the thumb until you have first stitched the hand outline. Cut head from skin-coloured fabric. Cut a $4\frac{1}{2}$" (11.5 cm) circle for the nose.

Place bow pattern on folded paper to make a complete pattern, then arrange it on the fabric with the centre to a fold so that you have one long bow strip. Cut a second bow in the same way to act as a lining. Cut a tie measuring 9" (23 cm)×4" (10 cm) from the remaining material.

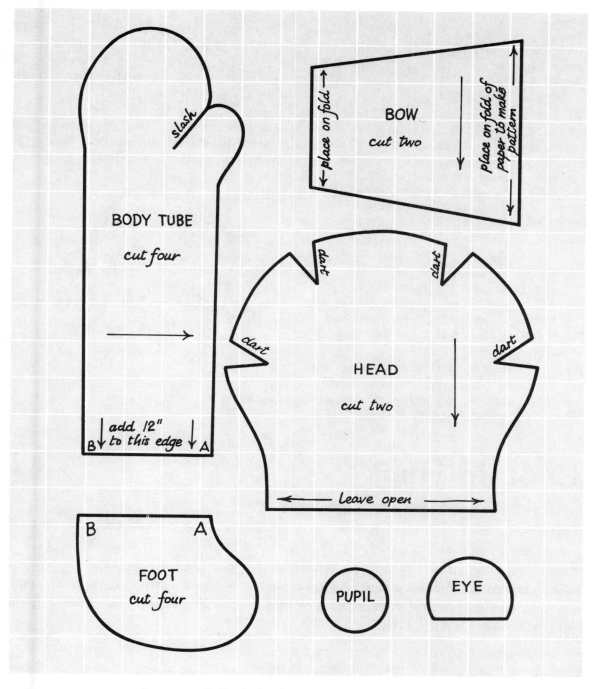

Pattern graph 23   Jotho the Clown *one square = 1″ (2·5cm)*

Match A and B of a foot and body tube piece and sew together on the wrong side. Prepare the other three pieces in the same way. Now place them together in pairs and sew each one on the wrong side, leaving an opening for turning. Slash the thumb, as marked on the pattern, and trim the upper foot curve. Turn each body tube right side out and stuff. Leave sufficient space at the opening so that the tubes can fold into arms and legs. Close openings with ladder stitch. Join the two tubes at the fold using a very strong linen thread.

93

Sew the four darts on both head pieces before sewing front and back heads together on the wrong side. Turn right side out and stuff firmly. Close the neck opening and sew head to shoulders with ladder stitch. Work two rows at least around the neck for strength.

Wind the wool into a 45″ (114 cm) hank and then cut it into 9″ (23 cm) lengths. Spread the wool out to make a block 10″ (25.5 cm) wide. Machine through the centre (see Figure 27, opposite). Arrange the wig so that the parting lies around the head in a typical clown style, leaving a bald top. Sew wig to head through the parting (see Figure 27), and then let the top half of the wig fall down to cover the stitching. Glue under the wig if you think it is necessary.

Arrange the felt eye shapes on the face and stick in position. Gather the outer edge of the felt nose circle, partially draw up, enclose a ball of stuffing in the centre and then close the nose. Sew to face.

Place right sides of both bow pieces together and sew along the top and bottom edges only. Turn right side out and press. Fold each half of the bow to bring the open ends together at the centre back. Stitch them together and at the same time gather up the centre of the bow. Fold the tie strip in half in both directions so that no raw edges are exposed. Now wrap tie over centre of bow and fasten on the back. Sew bow to neck of Jotho.

Groom your toy by trimming any uneven lengths of wool in the wig. You may even add bows or bells to the feet and ruffs around the ankles and wrists. Try experimenting.

Figure 27 Hair and facial features for Jotho

Captain Hook

This novelty doll is a further development of circle toys. Like the millipede, it has a body constructed from unstuffed circles which are threaded on elastic. It is somewhat difficult to estimate the exact amount of material needed for the circles, as you may decide on different colour combinations for the clothes. Captain Hook was of course a pirate. If you are making him for a very young child, replace the hook with a hand. You might even like to design a skull and crossbones hat for him.

Materials: 3½ yds (320 cm) of 36″ (91 cm) wide dress weight cotton
3 yds (274 cm) millinery elastic
5 large raincoat buttons
a 9″ (23 cm) square of black felt for boots and patch
4 ozs (112 g) stuffing
¼ yd (23 cm) of calico for head and hand
strip of yellow felt to cover hook
1 hook from a coat hanger
½ oz (13 g) double knitting (thick) wool for hair
felt for facial features
black wool or tape to tie patch
2 curtain rings for earrings
material for scarf

Cutting: Prepare patterns for head, hand, and boots from the pattern graph. You

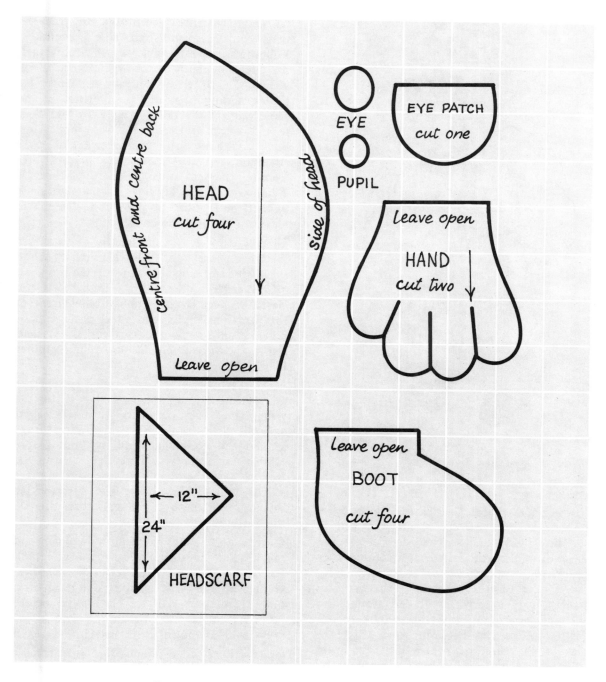

Pattern graph 24   Captain Hook *one square = 1″ (2·5cm)*

Cutting: (contd)	will also need circle templates cut from card with diameters of 8″ (20 cm), 6″ (15 cm), and 5″ (12.5 cm) respectively. This makes a pirate 18″ (46 cm) tall. Cut head and hand from calico. Do not slash between fingers until you have first stitched

them. Cut boots and patch from felt. Cut body circles as follows:—

   16 circles 8″ (20 cm) in diameter
   43 circles 6″ (15 cm) in diameter
   36 circles 5″ (12.5 cm) in diameter
Figure 28, page 96, shows how these circles are to be arranged.

Figure 28 Arrangement of circles for Captain Hook

Preparing the fabric circles for the body is rather a lengthy task so I suggest that you do this first by making a dozen or so at a time while sitting in the garden or watching television. In this way you can collect all the necessary circles together, ready for the final assembly. Run a gathering thread around the edge of each circle, pull up and fasten off. Flatten the circles between your fingers to make discs. Pierce the centre of each disc by pushing a steel knitting needle between the gathers and out through the smooth side of the disc. The elastic will be threaded through these holes.

Cut four 15″ (38 cm) lengths of elastic. Take just two of these lengths and tie the ends on to a raincoat button. This acts as an anchor, so the knot must be really secure. Now thread the free ends through a large darning needle and use this to pull the elastic through the

fabric circles. Thread 19 trouser leg circles on first, with the gathered side lowermost. Follow with the 4 trouser waist circles, then the circles of the body, chest, and neck. Look at Figure 28 to see the exact arrangement. Use the remaining two lengths of elastic in the same way for the other trouser leg and then thread it through the trouser waist circles and body circles alongside the other elastic. You should now have all four elastic ends emerging from the last neck circle. Tie these off through a raincoat button, leaving just enough slack so that the legs can be pulled and the elastic will be able to spring back.

Now cut two 18″ (46 cm) lengths of elastic for the arms. Tie two ends on to a button and then thread the free ends through a needle and push on 18 circles for the first sleeve. Pass the elastic between the two pairs of body elastic at the junction of the body and chest circles. Thread on 18 more circles for the second sleeve and tie off the elastic through another button.

Make the boots by placing each pair together and sewing around the curved edge on the wrong side. Trim curve and turn boots right side out. Stuff firmly. Run a gathering thread around the open edge, pull up, but before closing, push the button from the base of the trousers into the opening. Fasten off. Ladder stitch the first fabric circle of the trouser leg to the top of the boot for extra strength. Do this for both legs.

Place hands together with right sides facing and sew around the fingers. Slash between thumb and fingers and turn hand right side out. Stuff. Gather up the wrist opening and push in a button from the end of the sleeve before fastening off. Ladder stitch the first sleeve circle to the hand for extra strength.

Cut a strip of yellow felt and fold over the coat hanger hook. Slip stitch the edges together and bind the base of the hook with a little extra felt. Cut two yellow felt circles, large enough to cover the button at the end of the sleeve. Pierce the centre of one of these felt circles and push the base of the hook through it. Stitch securely in place. Sew the second felt circle to the first by oversewing the edge, enclosing a little stuffing as you work. Now place the prepared hook unit over the button at the end of

9 Dogs (opposite)
From top, moving clockwise : three versions of Bramble, Bones, Butter.

the sleeve and stitch the felt circles to the first fabric circle.

Sew the head pieces together in pairs by working the centre front and centre back seams first. Then sew the two halves together, leaving the neck edge open. Turn head right side out after trimming the curves. Stuff firmly. Cut the wool for the hair into 10″ (25·5 cm) lengths and then spread out to make a band 6″ (15 cm) wide. Machine through the middle to make a parting. Lay the wig on the head and sew in place through the parting. Spread some glue on either side of the head and press the sides of the wig down.

Cut an eye from felt pieces and stick on one side of the face. Attach tape to the eye patch or crochet a black chain for the tie. Place patch over the other eye position and fasten securely behind the head. Stick or stitch a mouth on the head. Decide whether you want a friendly or fierce mouth for your pirate and cut accordingly. Sew a curtain ring to each side seam where the ear would be.

The head is now ready to attach to the body. Gather up the neck edge and enclose the neck button in the opening before fastening off. This is rather tricky to do because of the weight of the head, so work stitches backwards and forwards through the button, elastic, and head to make really secure. Then, ladder stitch the first neck circle to the neck of the head to hide the join.

Make a narrow hem around the headscarf on all three sides. Put on head and tie at the back with a couple of knots. Finally, arrange the hair and trim any untidy ends.

Humpty Dumpty

One of the most popular nursery rhyme characters ever made as a toy is surely Humpty Dumpty. Young children love enacting the rhyme with him, making him fall down time and time again. He is just as popular with boys as with girls, which is very useful since it is often more difficult to make dolls for the former which will be acceptable.

With this in mind, I have included instructions for dressing Humpty Dumpty as a soldier. Although the body appears to be a simple shape for stuffing, be warned. Any irregularities in either sewing or stuffing are easily noticeable. You can make it easier for yourself by choosing a bold dark colour for the head and a gaily patterned fabric for the body, arms, and legs. I would strongly recommend that this toy be machined.

Materials:
$\frac{1}{3}$ yd (30 cm) of 48″ (122 cm) wide velvet
felt for eyes, nose, and mouth
$2\frac{1}{2}$ lbs (1135 g) stuffing
$\frac{1}{2}$ oz (13 g) thick knitting wool
$\frac{1}{2}$ yd (46 cm) of 48″ (122 cm) wide corduroy, printed needlecord, cotton rep, patterned furnishing weight cotton, tartan, etc.

Cutting:
Prepare a set of patterns from the graph, page 98. This makes a Humpty Dumpty 20″ (51 cm) tall. Cut four head pieces, two hands, two soles, and two pairs of boots from velvet. Do not slash the thumb before stitching, and take care that you read the instructions for cutting napped fabrics in Chapter One.
Cut two bodies, four side bodies, and two arms and legs from patterned fabric, remembering to reverse pattern when cutting pairs.

Velvet has a tendency to slip when stitching, so it is advisable to tack all pieces together first before sewing. Certainly you must not use pins, which damage the pile and leave marks.

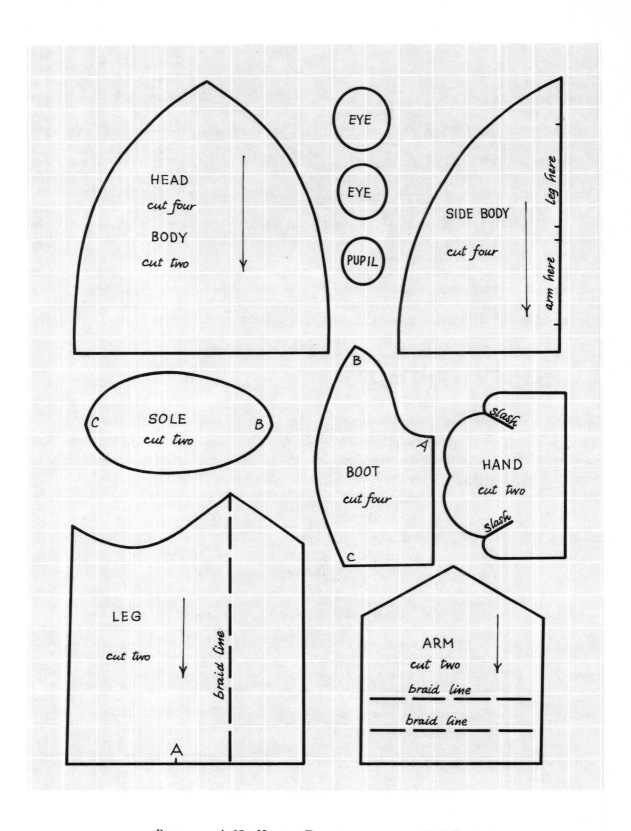

Pattern graph 25   Humpty Dumpty *one square = 1" (2·5cm)*

Tack two head pieces together on the wrong side along one curved edge, then sew. Repeat this with the other two head pieces. Now place both halves of the head together and tack, then sew, leaving the straight edges open. Turn right side out and carefully inspect the evenness of your seams. Select one of the head pieces to be the face.

Cut a circle of felt with a $3\frac{1}{2}''$ (9 cm) diameter. This is for the nose. Gather the circle around the raw edge and enclose a ball of stuffing before fastening off. Position nose on the centre line of the face segment, which you can determine by measuring from the side seams. It should be on the lower half of the face; look at the illustration facing page 81 if in doubt. Sew the nose securely to the face, for little fingers are sure to tug at it.

A commercial Humpty Dumpty often has a wool pompom for a nose which matches the wool of the hair. Although this solves the problem of matching colours, I feel that the nose is more likely to come apart and for this reason prefer the felt ball. When the nose is in place, you can use it as a marker to position the mouth and eyes. Decide whether you want to stitch or glue them down. The former is done at this stage while the latter is done on the finished toy. Gluing is an easier method of putting the features in the right place.

Make the hair by cutting the wool into $11''$ (28 cm) lengths. Tie them together in the centre, making two or three bundles altogether. Thread the ends of the ties on to a needle, pass through the top of the head, and tie off on the wrong side. Lay all the bundles as close together as possible and tug them to make sure that they are secure.

Tack a hand to the lower edge of each arm. Sew. Fold arm in half lengthways and sew around the fingers, between the thumb and along the straight edge of the arm. Leave the top open for turning. Slash between the thumb and fingers. Stuff each arm firmly, paying particular attention to the thumbs. Finish stuffing about $1\frac{1}{2}''$ (4 cm) from the top. Hold the stuffing away from the opening with either a pin or tacking stitches. Baste the open edges together.

Place a pair of boot pieces together, with right sides facing, and tack then sew A to B. Trim the curve and open the boots out. Place each boot against a leg, with right sides facing, and match A to A. Sew. Fold leg in half, lengthways, matching C to C of boot, and sew the centre back seam from C to the top of the leg, leaving the top open for turning. Insert sole, matching B to B and C to C. Tack, then sew. Turn leg right side out and stuff as for the arms. Finish the second leg in the same way. Place a side body to a body piece, matching the curved edge. Sew together on the wrong side. Sew another side body to the other side of the body piece in the same way. Now repeat all this with the remaining body and pair of side body pieces. You should now have two identical halves.

Baste arms and legs in position on the straight sides of one of the completed body halves. Now take up the other body half and lay it against the half with the arms and legs in place. Baste. Turn right side out to check that all the limbs are securely in place. This is very important and well worth taking the extra time and care to ensure a correct fit. When satisfied, machine the central seam several times.

The two halves, head and body, are now ready to put together. Make sure that both are inside out. Match the face segment to the front of the body by placing the seams together. Work all round in this way, matching seams wherever possible. The arm and leg seam will lie exactly halfway between two head seams.

Baste in position, then sew. Leave an opening in the centre back which is large enough to take your hand. Turn right side out and check the evenness of your sewing. I always like to sew the central join several times as it is under tremendous strain from both stuffing and the weaker edge of the velvet.

It takes a long time to stuff Humpty Dumpty correctly, so have plenty of patience and proceed carefully. Work from side to side and from head to body so that the toy is evenly moulded on all sides. Close the opening with ladder stitch. You might like to make a bow tie or collar to cover the join. Glue mouth and eyes in position. Finally, remove any pins or tacking stitches from the arms and legs and trim any uneven lengths of hair.

General Ben

Choose a coloured fabric for the body that suggests a uniform. Black felt can be used for the boots in place of the velvet. Apart from this you will need 2 yds (182 cm) of $\frac{1}{2}''$ (13 mm) wide gold braid, 8 uniform buttons, and 12" (30.5 cm) of gold lampshade fringe.

Follow the cutting and making instructions as given for Humpty Dumpty, with the following additions.

Sew strips of braid to legs and arms following guide line marked on pattern. Do this before you sew the hands or boots.

Arrange the buttons on front body and carefully measure their exact position before sewing them down.

Make a collar by cutting a strip of body fabric 2" (5 cm) wide, across the full width of the material. Fold in half with right sides facing and sew the short side and one long side. Turn right side out and iron. Sew braid around one long edge and both short edges. Position collar centrally between the head and body and baste, then sew.

Cut the lampshade fringe in half and fold raw edges under on both pieces. Lay each strip of braid over the top of an arm and sew in place.

13 Dogs

Dogs are the most variable of all the animals associated with man. Exactly when and how they became domesticated is rather difficult to determine, but it must have happened some 10,000 to 15,000 years ago. Perhaps it was the wolves which were first attracted to human camps by quantities of scrap meat and bones, and formed a loose association with the hunters in return for easy food. Then the children would have had an opportunity to adopt motherless puppies and abandoned weaklings just as the aboriginal children do with dingos even today. Many of these wolves would retreat to the wild as they grew up, but perhaps some stayed with the camps.

Constant interbreeding amongst dogs has meant that new breeds are being evolved all the time and that some very old breeds have died out altogether. We do not know the origin of many of our domesticated dogs. However, they are well established as 'man's best friend'. Bones, Bramble, and Butter are three friends for you to make. They are unidentifiable as breeds and yet are still recognizable as dogs, clearly illustrating the above point.

Bones

This little puppy is both simple and quick to make. Choose a gaily patterned cotton or knobbly textured cloth to make his body and a plain fabric of contrasting colour for the ear linings. In fact he can be made from any fabric, although his shape would be lost if made in a deep pile.

Materials:
$\frac{1}{4}$ yd (23 cm) of fabric
small piece of fabric for ear linings
6 ozs (170 g) stuffing
black and white felt for eyes

Cutting:
Make a set of pattern pieces from the graph, page 102. Bones stands 7″ (17.5 cm) tall from his toes to the tip of his tail. Cut body, underbody, and ears from main fabric, reversing the body to cut a pair. Cut two ear linings.

Make the ears first so that they are ready to machine on to the body. Place right sides of each ear lining and ear together. Sew round the outer curved edge. Trim and turn right side out. Make both ears in the same way. Press them both with an iron. Now place them together, like a sandwich, so that the linings are on the outside and the ears on the inside. Baste together along the open edge.

Take up one body piece with the right side facing you, lay the ears in place as indicated on the pattern, and sew. Now take up the second body piece and place it on top of the first. Sew from A to B and from C to D. The opening between B and C is for turning the skin through and stuffing. By doing it this way, the opening will be hidden under the ears in the finished toy.

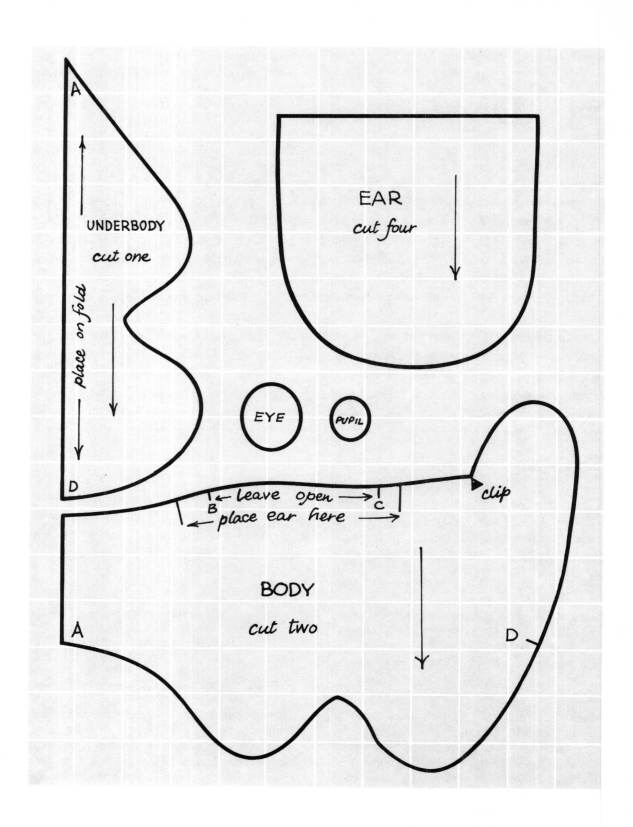

Pattern graph 26 Bones *one square = 1″ (2·5cm)*

102

Insert underbody, matching A to A and D to D. Baste. Sew one side first, then the other. Clip the tail and trim the curves between the legs. Turn skin right side out. Stuff Bones in the following order: tail, legs, bottom, snout, lower body, and lastly upper body. He must be really firm if he is to stand steady on his feet. Close opening beneath the ears.

Using double linen thread, make a giant cross stitch in each eye position. Work both sides at the same time so that you can pull up on the ends of the thread and tie them off together on one side. This will produce eye 'sockets', giving the head additional shaping. Glue pupils to the eyes, then the eyes to the head, so that they cover the stitches.

Bramble

Bramble is a simple dog to make, relying on colour and careful fitting together of the pattern pieces. He is designed specifically for making in fur fabric. His proportions suggest that he is a mischievous puppy – make him in any other fabric and he immediately becomes taller and therefore looks older.

Materials:
½ yd (46 cm) of 54″ (136 cm) wide fur fabric
12″ (30.5 cm) × 18″ (46 cm) white fur
pair of 20 mm safety eyes
10 ozs (280 g) stuffing
12″ (30.5 cm) braid
small buckle

Cutting:
Make a set of patterns from the graph, page 104, remembering to place the ear on folded paper to cut a complete pattern piece. This pattern makes a dog that sits 12″ (30.5 cm) high. Cut the front, back, base, lower feet, and outer ears from main coloured fur. Cut the ear linings, upper feet, and tail from white fur.

Commence with the front, by sewing both cheek darts on the wrong side. Then sew upper feet to the body, matching A to A and B to B of both pieces. Sew on the wrong side and trim the curve to ease the tension. Run an easing thread around the outer edge of both feet. This will be pulled up later to fit the curve of the lower feet.

Now place right sides of an ear and an ear lining together and sew around the edge leaving C to D to C open. Turn ear right side out and fold in half lengthways, bringing C to C. Lay ear in slit on body front, matching C to C and D to D. Baste, then sew, making sure that the ear is pushed away from the side seam allowance. Make the other ear in the same way.

Sew both head darts on the back, then place right sides of front and back together. Sew across the top of the head first, then down each side, checking that the ears are pushed well away from the seams. Fold tail in half, length-ways, and sew around the edge, leaving the base open. Turn right side out and lightly stuff. Baste tail to bottom edge of the centre back. Turn whole skin right side out and insert the eyes.

Take up the lower feet and sew them to the base, matching E to E and F to F. Turn body skin inside out and insert the base. Ease the upper feet to fit the lower feet. Sew the base in place, leaving an opening under the tail.

Turn the skin right side out again and stuff. Make sure that you give fullness to the cheeks and to the feet. Close opening with ladder stitch.

Attach braid to the buckle and then put around Bramble, just below the cheeks. Pull up tightly to form a neck. Sew collar securely in position. Make a block of satin stitches for the nose and finish Bramble by releasing any pile trapped in the seams and giving him a good brushing.

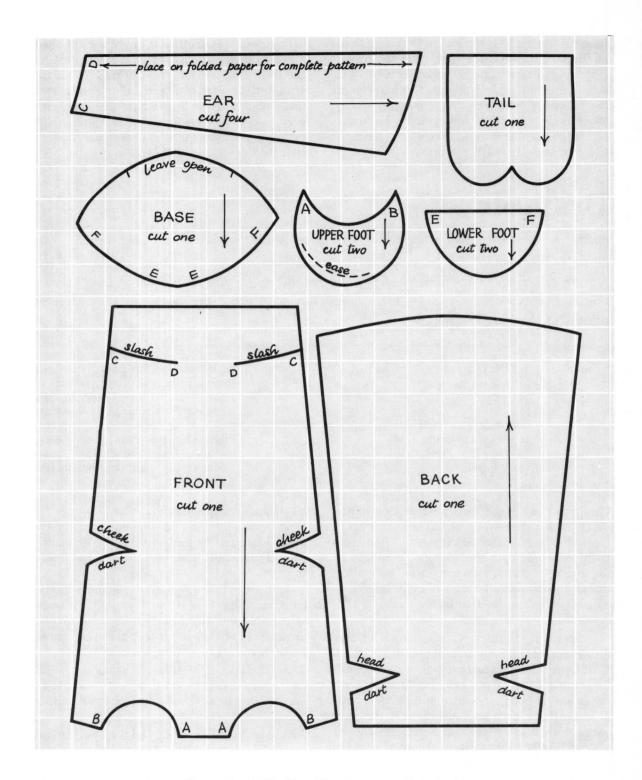

Pattern graph 27 Bramble *one square = 1″ (2·5cm)*

Further ideas for you to try

Give Bramble a completely new character by making him from a patterned furnishing weight cotton, bouclé, tweed, or even mohair. Make felt eyes when using these fabrics.

This pattern is suitable for either enlarging or reducing. The instructions for doing this are given in Chapter One.

Butter

To make this dog, I have chosen a rich yellow furnishing weight cotton fabric. His appeal is further enhanced by his sad eyes and drooping mouth which give him a doleful expression. Butter is perhaps the most difficult of the three dogs to make, as his skin requires careful stuffing if there are to be no unsightly bumps and wrinkles.

Materials: $\frac{2}{3}$ yd (61 cm) of 48″ (122 cm) wide patterned fabric
1 lb (454 g) stuffing
felt for eyes and nose
collar (optional)

Cutting: Prepare patterns from the pattern graph, page 106. Butter is 12″ (30.5 cm) long from nose to tail. Lay body pattern on the fabric and mark the cutting line of the hind leg with pencil. Do not slash this line until you have first stitched the body and underbody together. Cut two each of body, underbody, pairs of ears, and crown, remembering to reverse the pattern when necessary. Cut one only face, underchin, and tail.

Join the centre seam of the two underbodies on the wrong side. Leave an opening for turning the finished skin through. Open out and lay one body piece to the right side so that the legs are correctly matched together. Baste, then sew from A to B, passing on either side of the pencilled slash line for the hind legs.

Work a second row of stitching on top of the first to reinforce the seam. Now slash the hind leg free from the body. Join the second body to the opposite side of the underbody in the same way. Trim the seams around the paws.

Fold the tail in half, lengthways, and sew from the tip down to the base, leaving the end open. Turn right side out and stuff to within 1″ (2.5 cm) of the end. Place tail in position on one side of the centre back seam, with the tip facing inwards, and sew. Bring the centre back edges together and sew from the back to the neck edge, making sure that the tail is not in the way. Close and sew the short seam between A

and the neck. Put the body aside for the time being and make the head.

Start with the darts on the face. There are three in all – the crown, eye, and nose darts. The eye dart must be marked carefully so that it is symmetrical in the finished toy (see Figure 29, page 107).

Place two ear pieces together with right sides facing and sew the outer curved edge. Trim the seam. Turn ear right side out through the base. Press to remove any creases, then baste the raw edges together. Work second ear in the same way. Now fold each ear in half lengthways, and baste to the right side of the face where marked on the pattern.

Sew the centre seam of the crown on the wrong side from C to D. Place crown against face, matching C to the crown dart, and sew. Check that the ears are tucked away from the seam when sewing. Now is the time to hand sew or machine eyes in place if you so wish. Insert the

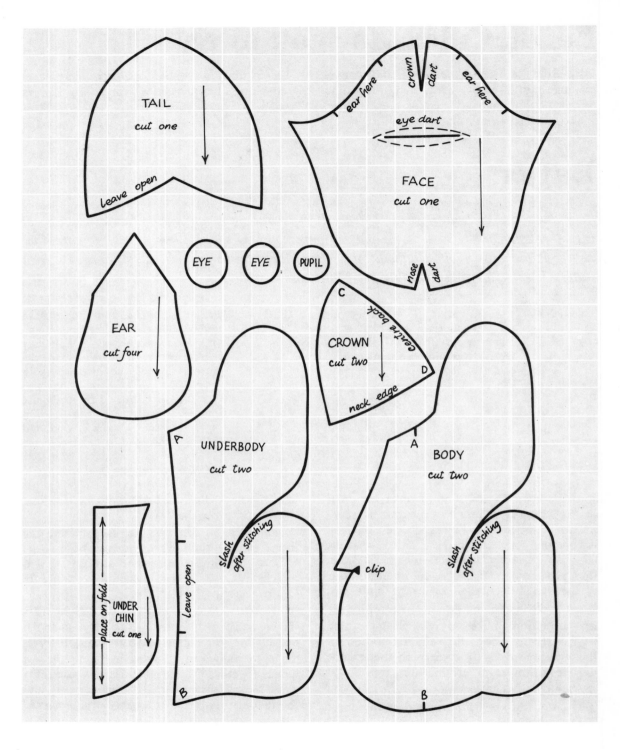

Pattern graph 28   Butter *one square = 1″ (2·5cm)*

106

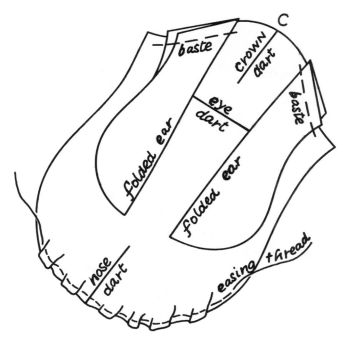

Figure 29 Detail of face construction for Butter

underchin, easing the face edge to fit, and sew. Turn completed head right side out and insert in neck opening of the body. Baste in position, matching D of crown to centre back seam of body. Sew. Turn the entire skin right side out through the opening in the underbody.

Stuff the head first, then each of the legs, and finally the main bulk of the body. Do this slowly and carefully for the reasons already mentioned. Close opening. The eyes may now be glued in place. To make the nose, cut a circle of felt with a 3″ (7.5 cm) diameter. Run a gathering thread around the edge, insert a ball of stuffing, then draw up the gathering thread tightly. Fasten off. Sew completed nose in position over the nose dart.

Further ideas for you to try

You might like to remake Butter as a sad-faced little lion. Cover the crown with loops of wool and sew a few of the loops on to the end of the tail. Redesign the ears and cut a long nose from felt.

Make Butter as a biscuit-coloured hound with darker felt patches appliquéd to his body surface, or as a dalmatian with a white body and black spots.

14   Bears

Incredibly, the establishment of the teddy bear as a popular toy dates from the beginning of this century, yet the exact nature of its origin is questionable. The name is in no doubt, as it is derived from the nickname of none other than President Theodore Roosevelt, who was portrayed in a cartoon with a bear in 1902. Bears are a widespread group of mammals, being found as polar bears in the far north, with species occurring throughout Europe and Asia, right down to the sun bear of Malaya and Indonesia. The tree bear, or koala, belongs to a very different group of animals, the marsupials, which are characteristic of Australia. Several designs for bears are included in this book. The two provided here are distinguished by their moveable limbs and the inclusion of a musical unit. The larger bear is jointed and the design of the head follows the more traditional patterns in having a long muzzle. In contrast, the musical bear has an anthropomorphic or humanized design with high forehead, rounded cheeks, and eyes facing forward. Although the arms and head are sewn in position, joints could be inserted without altering the pattern. Moreover, the choice of colour will affect the final appearance of the toy. For example, a pale colour will enhance the babyish appearance of the musical bear, while a dark colour will make the jointed bear suitable for an older child. The use of a deep pile fabric results in a very luxurious bear.

Musical Teddy

Read the instructions on inserting musical units in Chapter Two before making this toy.

Materials:
$\frac{1}{3}$ yd (30 cm) of 54″ (136 cm) wide fur fabric
12 ozs (340 g) stuffing
musical unit
pair of 16 mm safety eyes
dark thread for nose
ribbon for neck

Cutting: Make a set of patterns by enlarging those in the pattern graph. Place the body front to a folded edge to make a complete pattern. This makes a teddy that sits 11″ (28 cm) tall. Cut pieces from fur, reversing the patterns to cut pairs of head, arm, and side body pieces.

Commence by making the body. Sew the darts on the body front to shape the top of the legs. Place the two side bodies together with right sides facing and sew the centre back seam on either side of the opening. Now place all body pieces together, matching A to A, B to B, and C to C respectively. Baste, then sew. Clip all the corners as marked on the pattern, then turn the skin right side out. Stuff feet firmly, then legs and body. Close the neck with a running thread which can be partly drawn up for additional shaping at the shoulders. Insert the

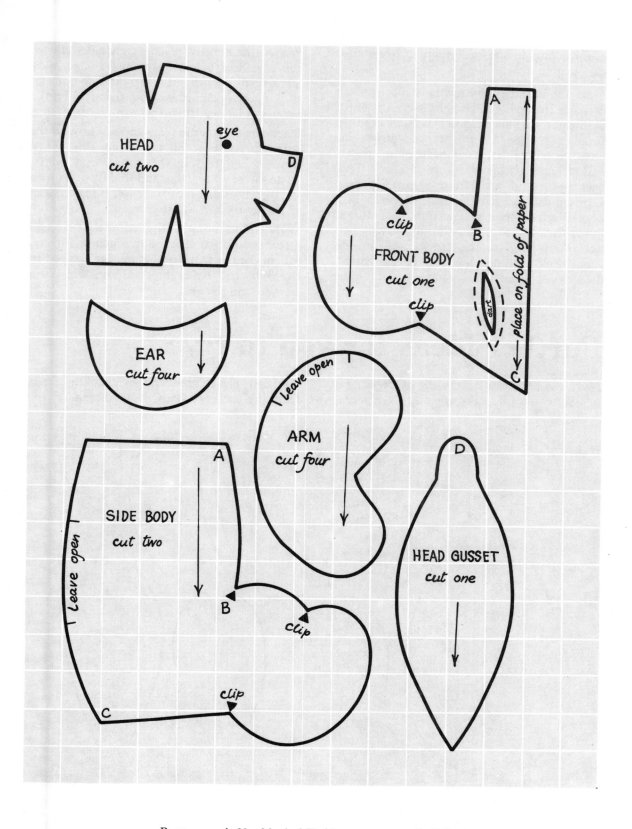

Pattern graph 29   Musical Teddy *one square = 1″ (2·5cm)*

musical unit in the back opening, then close the opening.

Make the head next by sewing the three darts on each side piece. Place the pieces together with right sides facing and sew from D to the front neck edge. Insert the head gusset and baste on both sides. Turn head right side out and check that this is evenly inserted. Turn back again and sew. Close remaining short seam at centre back of head, down to neck edge. Turn completed head right side out and insert the eyes. Stuff head firmly, paying particular attention to the cheeks and muzzle. Close neck opening with a gathering thread, then place head on shoulders and ladder stitch the two together.

Prepare the arms by placing right sides of each pair together, then sew around the edge, leaving a small opening. Turn right side out and stuff. Close opening. Position the arms on the body and ladder stitch them in place.

Place ears together in pairs and sew around the outer curved edge on the wrong side. Turn through and fold in the bottom raw edges. Baste the edges together and slightly pull up on the thread so that the ears 'cup'. Place on head and ladder stitch in place.

Work a block of satin stitches for the nose and a few straight stitches for the mouth. Finally, groom the toy by releasing any fur trapped in the seams and giving it a good brushing. Tie a bow around the neck.

Further ideas for you to try

Make the bear as a mascot toy by dressing in school colours with a cap and scarf or blazer.

The body can be used with several of the heads from the nursery toys, Chapter Seven.

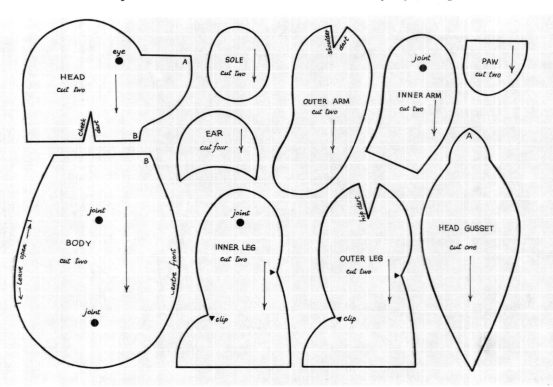

Pattern graph 30   Jointed Bear *one square = 1″ (2·5cm)*

110

Jointed Bear

Read the instructions for jointing in Chapter Two before making this toy.

Materials: ¾ yd (68 cm) of 54″ (136 cm) wide fur fabric
felt or leather for paws and soles
2 lbs (908 g) stuffing
2 joints for legs, each 2″ (5 cm)
2 joints for arms, each 1¾″(4.5 cm)
felt for eye backings
pair of 22 mm amber safety eyes
red ribbon and medallion (optional)
growler or squeaker (optional)

Cutting: Make a set of patterns from the pattern graph. This makes a teddy 20″ (51 cm) tall. Cut two paws and two soles from felt or leather. From the fur, cut a pair of every part except the head gusset, for which you will need only one, and the ears, for which you need two pairs. Mark position of joints on relevant pieces.

This bear consists of a series of completed units that have to be made individually before they can all be put together. Start by making the limbs. Each outer leg and arm has a dart which must be sewn on the wrong side. Sew paws to inner arms, then place both parts of each arm together with right sides facing and sew round the edge, leaving top open. Place both parts of each leg together in the same way and again sew, leaving the top and the base open. Insert sole in base and sew in place. Clip the corner at the top of the foot and turn all four limbs right side out. Stuff, insert joints, and close the openings.

Place both body pieces together with right sides facing and sew the centre front and centre back seam, leaving the opening in the back seam. Turn body skin right side out and finish jointing the limbs. Stuff the body, packing it carefully and firmly about the joints. Close the back opening and run a gathering thread around the neck opening. Pull up slightly and work a series of cross stitches across the neck to hold the stuffing in place.

Sew the darts on both head pieces then place them right sides together and sew the muzzle seam A to B. Insert head gusset, matching A to A, and baste to both sides of the head. Turn right side out and check evenness before sewing on the wrong side. Insert eyes. Cut a small circle of light coloured felt to place between eye and fur if you are making a dark coloured bear; this will serve to lighten the amber eye. Stuff head and gather up the neck edge. Place head on shoulders of body and ladder stitch the two together. Work around the join several times, each time with a separate thread.

Put the ears together in pairs and sew round the curved edge on the wrong side. Turn ears right side out and fold raw edges under. Baste the opening, then position ears on head and attach. Work a block of satin stitches for the nose and add a mouth. Finally, work over the seams, releasing any trapped fur. Tie a medallion around the neck for a champion bear.

15　The Seashore

Along the seashore can be found a wealth of different kinds of plants and animals, from sea-weeds to jellyfish, snails, and polar bears, but very few of these are ever made as soft toys. Included here you will find two birds, a mammal, and a crab.

Penguin

These swimming birds are typically thought of as inhabitants of the cold antarctic waters, but their distribution extends northwards to the tropics. This is the simplest of the seashore animals to make and is ideal for very young children.

Materials:　9″ (23 cm) × 30″ (76 cm) white fur
an 18″ (46 cm) square of blue, black, or brown fur
pair of 20 mm blue safety eyes
10 ozs (280 g) stuffing
felt for beak

Cutting:　Make a set of patterns from the pattern graph. This penguin is 12″ (30.5 cm) tall. Cut a pair of sides and wings and the head gusset from dark fur and the front, base, pair of wings, and face panels from white fur. Cut the beak pieces from felt.

Start by basting each face panel on to the wrong side of a body side, clipping the corner to make it easier. Sew. Now insert the small head gusset, matching A to A and B to B. Baste, then sew. Finish closing the centre back seam, B to C, leaving an opening for turning. Sew front face seam, A to D.

Insert front, matching D to D and E to E of side body. Sew on wrong side. Place the base in position, matching C to C and E to E on both sides. Sew. Turn completed skin right side out and insert safety eyes. Stuff body and close the back opening with ladder stitch.

Place a dark fur and white fur wing piece together with right sides facing and sew round the edge. Turn right side out and close opening. Sew wing to side of body around the top curve. Make a second wing in the same way and sew to the penguin.

Sew the two upper beak pieces together with a very narrow seam, then sew them to the lower beak. Turn right side out and stuff firmly. Place beak over front face seam and sew in place with tiny stitches. Finally, groom the penguin, being careful to release any fur trapped in the seams.

11 The Seashore (opposite)
From top, moving clockwise: puffin, penguin, puffin, crab, seal.

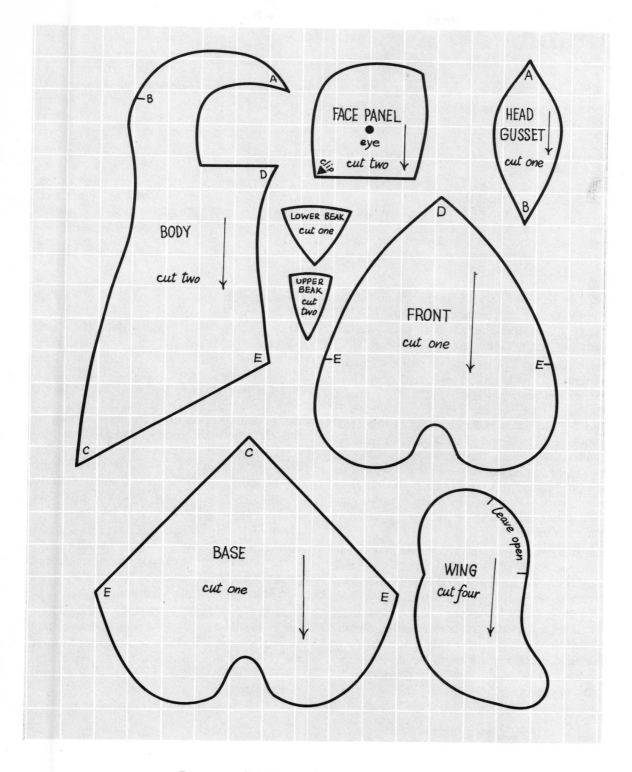

Pattern graph 31   Penguin *one square = 1″ (2·5cm)*

12 Wildlife and Lizards (opposite)
From top, moving clockwise : small version of lounge lizard, lounge lizard, hippopotamus, mother anteater, infant anteater.

Puffin

Puffins are fish-eating birds of the northern hemisphere, living on rocky coastlines with their nests in underground burrows on the grassy slopes of steep cliffs.

Materials:
9″ (23 cm) × 36″ (91 cm) felt for body
⅓ yd (30 cm) of 48″ (122 cm) patterned fabric
12″ (30.5 cm) square of red felt
1 lb (454 g) stuffing
black felt and bell for collar (optional)

Cutting:
Make a set of patterns from the pattern graph. This makes a puffin which is 12″ (30.5 cm) tall. Cut four feet, two eyes, and two beaks from red felt. Cut two bodies, head, and one back gusset from patterned fabric. Cut underbody, two sides, and two cheeks from large piece of felt.

Start by basting a felt side to the wrong side of a body, taking care to match A, B, and C. Clip the corner of the side pieces so that you can turn neatly. Sew. Repeat for the other side.

Now place back gusset to one side of body, matching D to D and E to E, and sew. Place the second body to the other side of the gusset and sew. Close centre back seam between E and F. The underbody can now be inserted, matching G to G and D to D on both sides. It is advisable to baste this first to make sure that you have a good fit. Any excess gusset can be trimmed away at D. Sew underbody and close short seam, D to D. The body is now completed and ready for the head to be inserted before stuffing.

Lay a felt cheek on the right side of a fabric head and top stitch it in place round the entire edge with the straight stitch of your machine. Use a contrasting thread for this, say yellow. Lay the beak on top of the cheek and straight stitch the outer edge to act as a basting thread. I used the zig zag stitch of my machine to sew the inside edge of the beak to the cheek and to work a row of colour down the cheek, just in front of the eye. If you do not have a zig zag

machine, either work several rows of straight stitch very close together or embroider with a fancy stitch of your choice. Make both head pieces in the way described, then place them right sides together and sew forward from H to I. Leave the neck between H and I open. Turn head right side out and check that the beak is securely stitched along the front edge. Push head through neck opening of body so that right sides are together and F is matching I. H will match the mid point of the underbody. Sew round neck several times. Turn completed skin right side out through opening in underbody. Stuff head first, particularly the neck, then the tail and body. Close opening.

Place each pair of feet together and sew the outside edge, leaving a small opening. Clip corners and turn right side out, stuff, and close opening. Ladder stitch to underbody and side so that puffin stands balanced.

Stab stitch the pupils to the eyes and then hem the eye to the cheeks, inserting a little stuffing as you work so that the eyes are raised above the cheeks. Cut a black felt strip to pass round the neck and join the two ends with a small nickel plated bell.

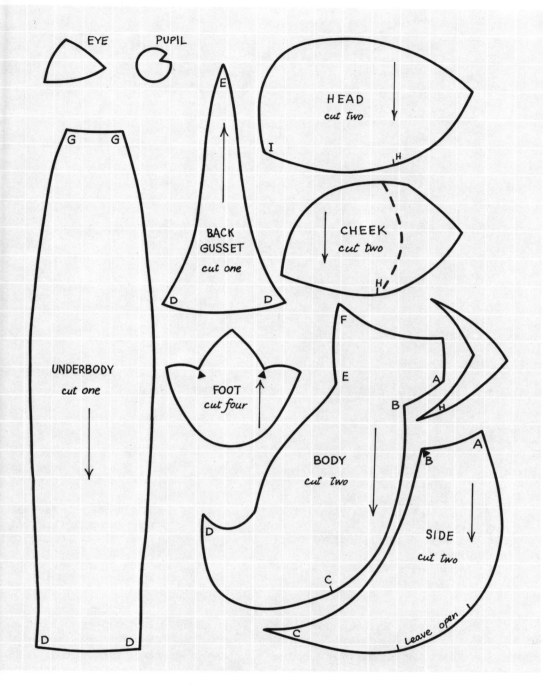

Pattern graph 32   Puffin *one square = 1″ (2·5cm)*

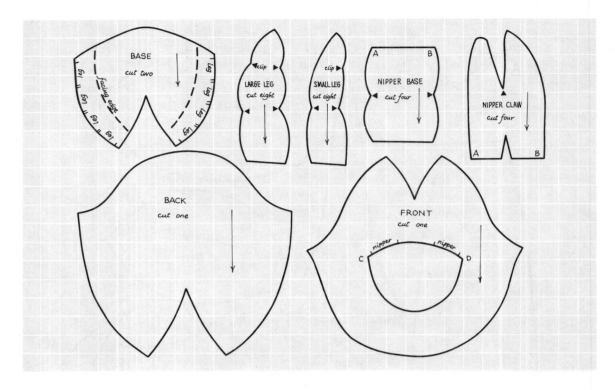

Pattern graph 33   Crab *one square = 1″ (2·5cm)*

Crab

Materials: $\frac{2}{3}$ yd (61 cm) of 48″ (122 cm) wide
patterned fabric
1$\frac{1}{4}$ lb (566 g) stuffing
12″ (30.5 cm) × 1$\frac{1}{2}$″ (4 cm) felt for
eye stalk
2 circles of white felt 3$\frac{1}{2}$″ (9 cm) in
diameter
small pieces of coloured and black
felt for pupils

Cutting: Make a set of patterns from the
pattern graph. This makes a crab
measuring 9″ (23 cm) across the
back. Cut one only back and front,
two base pieces, two pairs of nippers,
and four pairs each of large and small
legs. You should have 28 pieces in all,
not counting the eyes.

Collect all the leg pieces together and lay them
out in groups of large legs, small legs, and
nippers. Place each pair of large legs together
and, with right sides facing, sew a narrow seam
round the outer curved edge. Clip corners,
turn right side out, and stuff to within 1$\frac{1}{2}$″
(4 cm) of the opening. Hold stuffing away
from the opening with a few large tacking
stitches. Make all the large and small legs in
this way.

Sew the dart on the nipper claw first, then sew
claw to nipper base, matching A and B. Place

right sides of each nipper together and sew
round the edge, leaving base open. Clip
between the claws and turn right side out.
Stuff and finish as you did for the other legs.
Baste the open edges together and slightly
draw up. Now place base of nippers to front
as marked on pattern and, with claws facing
outwards, sew securely in place.

Make the dart on both base pieces. Now lay
bottom of legs to each side of one base piece,
with the claw ends pointing inwards. The large
legs lie in front of the smaller legs and there

116

should be two of each on either side. Baste, then sew. This is awkward because there are so many legs to fit in. Push them close together if necessary and also make them progressively shorter by sewing in more of the base of each leg.

The second base is laid over the first and then sewn to it round the leg edge so that the legs are sandwiched between the two. Turn base pieces right side out to free the legs. Select one side as being the neatest, then cut away the other so that it now acts as a facing. The cutting line for the facing edge is marked on the pattern.

Sew the central shaping dart on both front and back pieces, then place them together with right sides facing and sew all round the outer edge. Trim the curves and turn right side out. Place base to body front, matching C to C and D to D. Baste, then sew, checking that the nippers are securely caught in the seam and that no basting stitches are visible.

Stuff the skin and cover the opening by folding the base over and ladder stitching it to the front. Your stitches should pass through the base facing fabric, on the very edge just beneath the legs.

Cut the eye stalk felt in half lengthways and roll each one up tightly to make the stalk. Slip stitch the edge. Gather up edge of white eye felt and insert a ball of stuffing before closing. Sew each eyeball to an eye stalk. Cut a two coloured pupil for each eye and glue to the eyeball.

Seal

Seals are found in all the oceans of the world and even in one large freshwater lake in Russia. An imitation sealskin fabric in coating quality has been used to make this toy. The seal, however, would look equally attractive in other fur fabrics and tweed cloths. Instructions are given for adapting the pattern to other fabrics.

Materials: 19″ (48 cm) × 29″ (73.5 cm) white fur
pair of 22 mm blue safety eyes
1 lb (454 g) stuffing
horsehair whiskers (optional)

Cutting: Make the pattern from the pattern graph, page 118. This seal is 19″ (48 cm) from nose to tip of flippers. Lay pattern according to the layout guide and cut two bodies, two flippers, and one each underbody and head gusset.

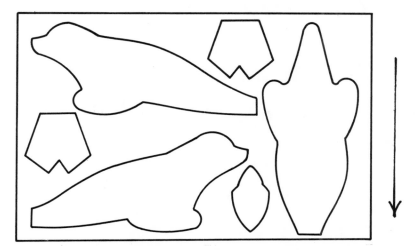

Figure 30 Pattern layout for seal. The arrow indicates direction of pile or grain of fabric.

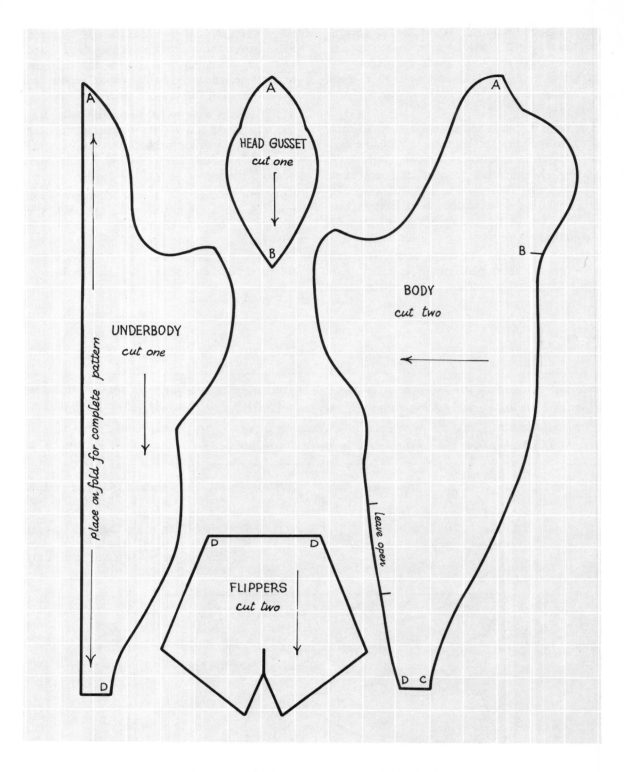

HEAD GUSSET
cut one

UNDERBODY
cut one

place on fold for complete pattern

BODY
cut two

A

B

leave open

D C

FLIPPERS
cut two

D   D

A

D

Pattern graph 34   Seal *one square = 1″ (2·5cm)*

118

If you are using a very heavy fur, do trim or shave the pile away from the seam allowance, otherwise there will be too much bulk for your machine.

Commencing with one body piece and the head gusset, place both right sides together, matching A. Baste in position, working round the curve of the head to B. Repeat on the other side. Turn fur right side out to check that the gusset is inserted correctly. If this is uneven, the head will be lopsided and misshapen, thus spoiling the final appearance of the toy. Now turn fur inside again and sew along the basting on both sides, remembering to break the stitching at A. Starting at B, sew the centre back seam, B to C.

Baste underbody to both sides of body. Check that it is properly inserted, as you did for the head gusset. Sew on the wrong side, again working carefully around A so as not to spoil the shape. Leave an opening along one side for stuffing, as indicated on the pattern. Turn skin right side out and insert eyes now. Stuff the body by starting with the head and working backwards. Keep the contours smooth so that the head sits above the front feet. Close the stuffing opening with ladder stitch.

Place the flippers together with right sides facing. Sew the outer edge, leaving D to D open. Clip deeply into the cleft and then turn flippers right side out. Using double linen thread, gather up the opening. Now match D and D of flippers to D and D of body. Sew together with ladder stitch and work around the opening at least twice. Any extra stuffing needed in the body can be added just prior to finally closing.

If wired or felt eyes are being used, now is the time to attach them. As a further finishing touch you might like to add a small group of whiskers to either side of the face. Finally, groom the toy by releasing any fur trapped in the seams and giving the body a good brushing.

Further ideas for you to try

This seal could be made in a printed cloth, tweed, or wool. If you do this then the pattern must be altered so that the flippers can be machined to the body. Redraw the body and underbody patterns so that the distance between C and D and D and D is equal to the distance D and D of the flippers.

Stitch the outer edge of the flippers, clip the cleft and turn right side out. Make the rest of the seal as already described up to the point of stuffing, but leave the skin inside out. Push the flippers through the body opening so that the two right sides are facing and, with D to D matching, machine in place. Now turn the complete skin right side out through the opening left for stuffing.

Stuff and close with ladder stitch.

16 Wildlife

All those animals not kept by man, either for his benefit or as pets, are usually referred to as wildlife. There are many examples already provided in the book, but here are a few rather unusual animals designed as toys.

Mother Anteater with Infant

Anteaters are found only in South America, the largest species being nearly five feet long. Anteaters also have long tails which they use to fold over their bodies like blankets when sleeping. However, the tail is missing from the toy, as it has been designed for sitting as a large dumpy animal.

Materials:
2 oz (56 g) rug wool or very thick knitting wool
⅔ yd (61 cm) of 54″ (136 cm) wide bouclé or similar fabric with an interesting texture
2½ lbs (1135 g) stuffing
an 18″ (46 cm) square of felt for ears and fingers
white fur for eyes
black felt for eyes
small piece of stiffener or interfacing for ears

Cutting:
Make the patterns by enlarging those shown in the graphs, pages 121 and 122. The mother is 18″ (46 cm) tall and the infant 6″ (15 cm) tall.
For the infant, you will need to cut a pair of body pieces and ears and one base from bouclé. Cut a pair of ear linings and fingers from felt and a base from stiff cardboard.
For the mother, you will need to cut one body placed to a fold, one front, base, and a pair of ears from the bouclé. Two arms and two feet will also be needed, but these are not cut as pairs.
Cut a pair of ears and two sets of fingers from the felt and lastly, a pair of ears from some stiffening material.

Commence making the infant by cutting the wool for the mane. Cut several 2″ (5 cm) lengths from the hank and lay them side by side until you have a band that is 3½″ (9 cm) long. Sew along the edge of the band, just catching the edges together. Lay the stitched edge on the right side of one body piece, matching A and B so that the band is directed towards the front of the body. Sew. Now place the second body piece on top of the first, with right sides together, and sew from the base at the back along the mane, the snout, and down the centre front to the base again. Turn right side out and gently tug at the mane to make sure that it is secure. Stuff the infant, paying particular attention to the neck. Leave the base open for the moment.

Take up the fabric base and run a double linen thread around the raw edge. Place the stiff card in the centre of the fabric base and pull up on the thread so that it moulds over the card. Insert base on the stuffed infant and ladder stitch the two together.

Make each ear by sewing the two pieces together on the wrong side, leaving the base open. Turn right side out and fold the raw edges under. Slip stitch these closed, and ladder stitch the ears to the head.

Roll up each finger strip of felt and catch at the base with a few stitches, then sew to the front of the body. Make the eyes by cutting two small circles of white fur and running a gathering thread around the raw edge. Pull up to form a ball but do not stuff. Flatten the fur with your fingers to make discs, then sew one of these discs to each eye position. Stick the black pupil in place. Finish the infant anteater by trimming the mane to give a pleasant shape.

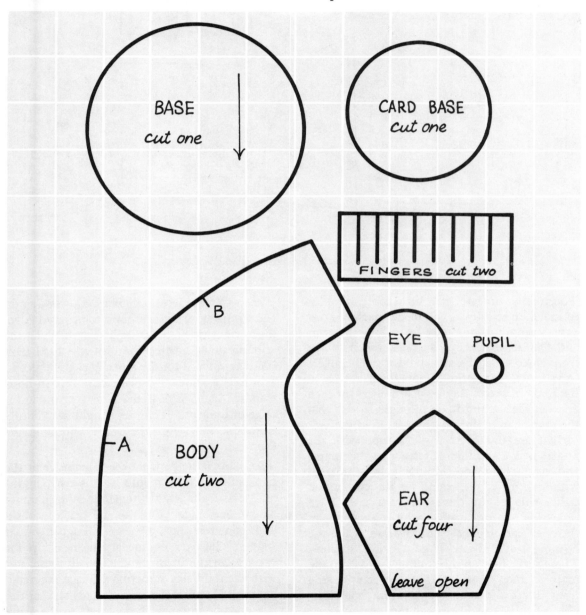

Pattern graph 35   Infant Anteater *one square = 1″ (2·5cm)*

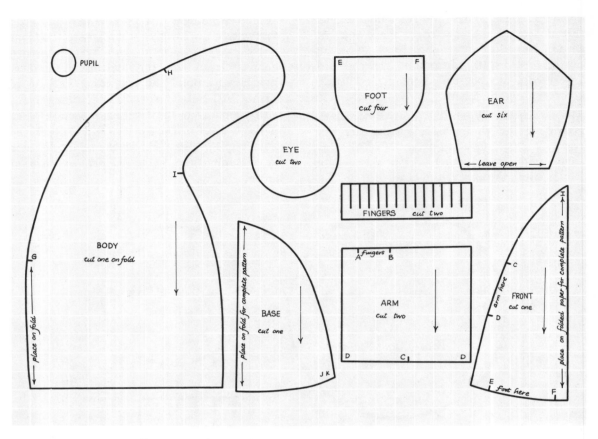

Pattern graph 36   Mother Anteater *one square = 1″ (2·5cm)*

The mother anteater is a little more complex to make and really needs to be machined for extra strength. Commence by making the arms and feet so that they can be stitched to the front as completed units. Fold the felt fingers in half, twice, and stitch across the base to hold the folds in place. Lay a set of fingers on each arm between A and B, on the right side so that the fingers are pointing inwards. Fold the arm in half lengthways to make a tube with the fingers inside and then stitch across the fingers and up the long side. Although the arm is cut with straight edges, round off the corners on either side of the fingers as you sew. Turn right side out and stuff to within 2″ (5 cm) of the open end. Hold the stuffing away from the opening with a few large tacking stitches. These serve to keep the stuffing away from the machine foot when you sew the arms to the front. Place the arms on the front, matching C to C and D to D so that they are directed inwards, and sew.

Place two feet pieces together and, working on the wrong side, stitch around the curved edge. Turn right side out and lightly stuff. Push the stuffing down against the toes and hold it in place as you did for the arms. Make the second foot in the same way. Place both feet in position, matching E to E and F to F at the lower edge of the front. The toes should be pointing upwards. Sew. Put the front aside for the moment.

The mane is made from the remainder of the hank of wool. Cut it into 3″ (7.5 cm) lengths and sew all the lengths together by machining across one edge. This should make a strip approximately 14″ (35·5 cm) long. I would suggest that you double stitch the strip for extra security. Open the main body piece out with the right side uppermost. Place the mane between G and H on one side only so that the free ends lie inwards. Baste, then sew the mane to the body.

122

Now fold the body in half so that the mane is inside, and sew from G to H and around the head to I. Double stitch this seam. Turn skin right side out and tug at the mane to make sure that it is really secure. Turn inside out again and attach the front, then the base, always working on the wrong side. Make sure that the arms are tucked away from the machine foot and that you leave the straight edge, J to K, open for stuffing. It is advisable to put in a row of stay stitching between J and K to stop the material from fraying while you stuff the toy. Turn right side out and start stuffing from the snout at the tip of the head. It is most essential that the anteater is adequately stuffed to prevent the neck collapsing and the head sagging to one side. Therefore work the stuffing in slowly and evenly against the stuffing already in position. This can take a long time. Close the opening with ladder stitch, working along the opening twice with separate threads.

Each ear consists of three pieces: the fabric, felt lining, and interfacing. Lay all the pieces in front of you, remembering that the ears are cut as a pair, with one side being reversed. Starting with the right side of a fabric piece facing you, lay a felt lining on top and then an interfacing. Sew round the outer curved edge, leaving the straight edge open. Trim the seams and cut the point off the tip of the ear. Turn right side out and fold under the raw edges. Stitch them together with ladder stitch and pull gently on the thread so that the ear becomes cup-shaped. Make the second ear in the same way. Now place both ears on the head of the anteater, moving them around until you are happy with their appearance. Note that the variations in the position of the ears and the eyes change the character of the mother, therefore it might be wise initially to pin them in place. Catch in position with ladder stitch.

The eyes are made from slightly stuffed fur circles. Run a linen gathering thread around the outer edge of the fur circle and gently pull up, inserting a little stuffing as you work. Attach the pupil slightly off centre with slip stitch. Make the second eye in the same way. Hold the eyes to the toy, moving them around until you feel happy with the expression obtained. Sew securely in place. Stitch the nostrils to the end of the snout, using the seams as a guide line to get them even. To groom this toy trim the mane and remove any tacking stitches from the feet and arms.

Hippopotamus

The favourite haunt of the hippopotamus is the water and the large bulbous eyes and nostrils situated high on the head enable it to remain submerged for most of the day. The head of this pattern identifies the toy as a hippo while the pattern for the body could be equally well used for any other bulky mammal.

Materials: 18″ (46 cm) × 30″ (76 cm) wide fur fabric
small piece of white fur for body gusset
12 ozs (340 g) stuffing
2 joints for arms, each 1¼″ (3 cm)
white cotton for sewing eyes
small pieces of black felt and coloured felt for pupils
dark wool for mouth

Cutting: Make the patterns from the pattern graph, page 124. The hippo stands 12″ (30.5 cm) high. Cut the body gusset from white fur and all the other parts of the body from main colour fur, remembering to reverse the patterns when cutting the second member of a pair.

Start by making the shoulder dart in each side body and body gusset. Match inner legs, placing them right sides together, and sew from A to B. Now insert body gusset and sew C to D. Sew the other side of the body in the way just described and finish sewing body

123

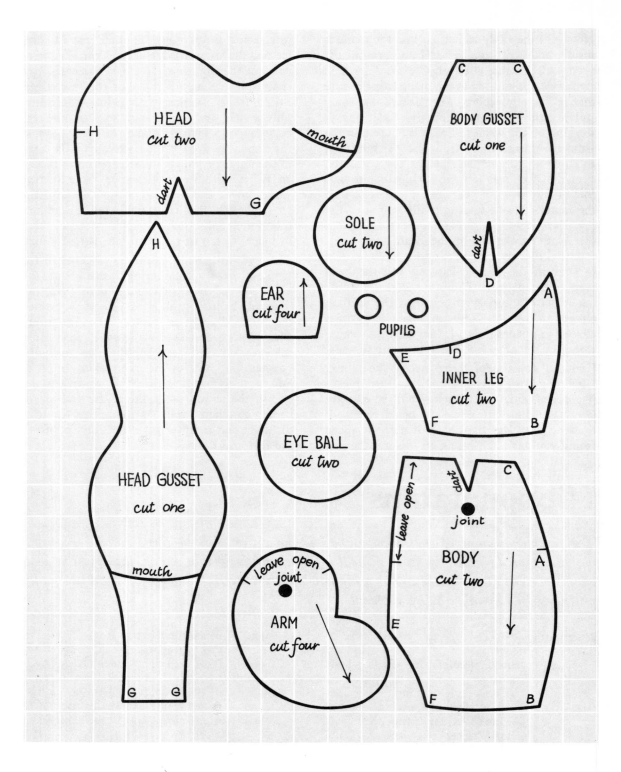

Pattern graph 37 Hippopotamus *one square = 1" (2·5cm)*

124

gusset in place. Finish the short seam between D and E. Fold the body in half so that the centre back seam is formed. Leave the first part open for stuffing and make a small seam down to E. You will now be able to sew the back leg seams from E to F on both sides, working from F and breaking the stitching at E so as not to catch the seam. Insert each sole and sew in place on the wrong side.

Make the dart in both head pieces, then insert the head gusset between them, matching G and H. Baste. Check for evenness, then sew. Close the remaining head seam from H to neck edge. Stuff the head firmly and run a gathering thread around the neck to hold the stuffing in place. Make the ears by sewing around the outside edge of each pair on the wrong side. Turn right side through, fold in half and sew to the top of the head, just behind the eye position.

Place a pair of arms together with right sides facing and sew, leaving the top open. Read the instructions for jointing in Chapter Two and finish the arm accordingly. Joint arms to the body. The body is now ready for stuffing. Work into the legs first, then the body proper. Close the back opening and gather up the neck edge to hold the stuffing in place. Place head on shoulders and ladder stitch the two together.

Gather the raw edge of the eyeball and insert a ball of stuffing before pulling up and fastening off. Sew eyeball to head and glue a pupil in place. Make second eyeball in same way.

The eyelids are made by cutting two strips of fur, 4″ (10 cm) long by 2″ (5 cm) wide. Fold the raw edges under then sew a strip over each eyeball. Work a mouth in wool. This is simply a very long straight stitch that passes from side to side in a curve beneath the nostrils. It can be caught down as it passes over each side of the gusset. Finish the hippopotamus by giving it a brushing and releasing any fur trapped in the seams.

17 Lounge Lizard

Throughout the tropics there is a small lizard that inhabits the living-rooms of houses, running up walls, across ceilings and hiding behind pictures. This is the gecko. This lizard can be considered either as a very large soft toy or as a piece of furniture on which children can play.

Materials: 3½ yds (320 cm) of 48″ (122 cm) wide strong fabric
a 3 pint can of Polybeads (if not available, use 10 lb (4.5 kg) foam chips)
2 lbs (1 kg) foam chips
3 lbs (1.5 kg) kapok or general toy filling
2 circles of fur for eyes 6″ (15 cm) in diameter
felt for eyes

Cutting: Make the patterns from the pattern graph. Lay both top and base pieces on folded paper to cut a complete pattern. This makes a lounge lizard nearly 54″ (136 cm) long. Cut all pieces from fabric, remembering to reverse the pattern when pairs are needed. The yardage given allows you to match a patterned fabric.

Place right sides of top and one side piece together and sew from A to B. Place second side to the top and again sew from A to B. Double stitch these seams for extra strength. Insert the base and sew from A to B on both sides. Again you will need to double stitch the seam, and remember to leave an opening on one side. Trim seams over the eyebrow curve and turn skin right side out.

Pour in ready prepared granules and half the foam chips. Hold the opening closed with a bull dog clip and shake the lizard vigorously to mix the stuffings. Foam chips may be used in place of Polybeads, but this rather detracts from the appearance of the toy. Continue until the skin is bulked out, but not rigid. Close opening.

Each limb is made in the same way. Sew the two darts on the outer piece on the wrong side. Lay right sides of an outer and an inner limb together and sew round the edge. As you go, ease the top curve to collect in the fullness. Clip points of toes and between the toes. Turn right side out and stuff firmly with kapok or similar fibre. Foam chips can be used mixed with the fibre, but not on their own, as they spoil the appearance. Close opening and position limb against the side body. Join with a circular row of ladder stitch. Sew a second row outside the first; you will be able to pull up tighter on this row and obtain a closer fit. Fasten off securely.

Run a gathering thread around the raw edge of the fur circle. Pull up, inserting a little stuffing for shaping. Sew felt eye to fur, then glue pupil to the felt eye. Ladder stitch the eye to the head just beneath the eyebrow bulge. Make second eye in the same way.

If you would like a more modest sized lizard, redraw the pattern on one inch squares. This makes a toy 27″ (68.5 cm) long. In this case you will only need 1 yd (91 cm) of 48″ (122 cm) wide fabric and 1¾ lb (794 g) stuffing. Follow the instructions for the large lizard but stuff firmly and cut new eye shapes. **There is no need for fur circles in the smaller version.**

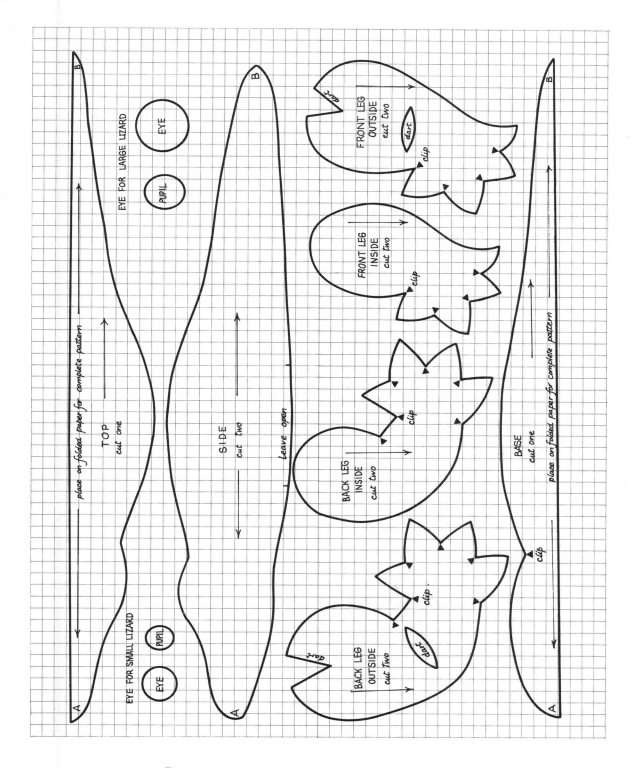

The following labels appear within the pattern graph:

B

EYE FOR LARGE LIZARD

EYE

PUPIL

place on folded paper for complete pattern

TOP
cut one

SIDE
cut two

Leave open

A

EYE FOR SMALL LIZARD

PUPIL

EYE

A

B

FRONT LEG
OUTSIDE
cut two

dart

clip

FRONT LEG
INSIDE
cut two

clip

BACK LEG
INSIDE
cut two

clip

BACK LEG
OUTSIDE
cut two

dart

clip

clip

BASE
cut one

clip

place on folded paper for complete pattern

B

A

Pattern graph 38   Lounge Lizard *one square = 1″ (2·5cm)*

127

Index